ACTIVE INVESTING IN THE AGE OF DISRUPTION

ACTIVE INVESTING IN THE AGE OF DISRUPTION

The Confluence of Central Bank Intervention and Technology Acceleration

Evan L. Jones

WILEY

Published by John Wiley & Sons, Inc., Hoboken, New Jersey.
Published simultaneously in Canada.

For general information on our other products and services or for technical support, please contact our Customer Care Department within the United States at (800) 762-2974, outside the United States at (317) 572-3993 or fax (317) 572-4002.

Wiley publishes in a variety of print and electronic formats and by print-on-demand. Some material included with standard print versions of this book may not be included in e-books or in print-on-demand. If this book refers to media such as a CD or DVD that is not included in the version you purchased, you may download this material at http://booksupport.wiley.com. For more information about Wiley products, visit www.wiley.com.

Library of Congress Cataloging-in-Publication Data

Names: Jones, Evan L., author.
Title: Active investing in the age of disruption / Evan L. Jones.
Description: Hoboken, New Jersey : Wiley, 2020. | Includes index.
Identifiers: LCCN 2019057707 (print) | LCCN 2019057708 (ebook) | ISBN
  9781119688082 (hardback) | ISBN 9781119688075 (adobe pdf) | ISBN
  9781119688129 (epub)
Subjects: LCSH: Investments. | Portfolio management.
Classification: LCC HG4521 .J665 2020 (print) | LCC HG4521 (ebook) | DDC
  332.6–dc23
LC record available at https://lccn.loc.gov/2019057707
LC ebook record available at https://lccn.loc.gov/2019057708

Cover Design: Wiley
Cover Image: © Holmes Su/Shutterstock

Printed in the United States of America

V10018019_031320

CONTENTS

ABOUT THE AUTHOR

Evan L. Jones oversees direct investments for Duke University Management Company (DUMAC) and teaches a course on investment management and endowments.

DUMAC manages $19 billion on behalf of Duke University and affiliates investing globally across all asset classes. Direct investments span global equities, commodities, credit, and market-neutral strategies.

Prior to joining DUMAC, Evan cofounded and managed Brightleaf Partners, a long/short US equity hedge fund. Brightleaf Partners focused primarily on consumer micro-cap companies and managed assets for high net worth and institutional investors.

Prior to Brightleaf Partners, Evan founded and was chairman/CEO of TSI Soccer, a catalog and e-commerce retailer focused on soccer enthusiasts. TSI Soccer was one of *Inc. Magazine*'s 500 fastest-growing companies in the US for two consecutive years (1993–1994). TSI Soccer distributed seven million catalogs, operated 12 retail stores, and created one of the sporting goods industries' first e-commerce sites. TSI Soccer was sold to a publicly traded company (Delias: DLIA) in 1998.

Evan has taught at Duke University since 1998 (entrepreneurship and investment management).

He is a graduate of Duke University (BA 1987), University of North Carolina Kenan-Flagler (MBA 1993), and is a CFA charter holder.

ACKNOWLEDGMENTS

Thank you to all my colleagues at Duke University Management Company. Your experiences and insights have made me a better investor and keep me thinking in new ways. Special thanks to Neal Triplett, CIO, and the direct investments team (John Burkert, Brandon Gall, Ian Jennings, and William Hockett) for their insights and camaraderie in battling the markets on a daily basis.

Thank you to John Pinto, my cofounder and partner at Brightleaf Partners. Running a small cap hedge fund for seven years that culminated in the extreme volatility of the great financial crisis should have been enough to force us both into retirement, but you never stopped looking for the next great idea. Your enthusiasm for investing is unparalleled.

Thank you to all my Duke students for keeping me young and curious, which is important in a profession in which the turmoil of the markets can make you old and fatalistic fast.

Last, thank you to my family—Suma, Kiran, Morgan, and Dylan—for always being the brightest part of my life.

PREFACE

Why write this book?

There are thousands of research and thought pieces written every day across the investment industry. Investment professionals get hundreds of emails each day with news and opinions on the market. They can listen to podcasts and watch television every moment of the day, only to wake up the next day and get a new stream of data and opinions. Brilliant, educated analysts; pundits; and executives offer their market opinions all day every day. It is pumped into investment firms like a firehose in the hope of finding an edge to make better decisions and outperform the market. However, the information is almost always in the context of the current point in time and never filtered by any screen of relevance or importance to the specific investment mission.

Information is of value only if investors have a very clear understanding of their investment process and what is truly informative to an investment decision. A detailed, disciplined investment process is necessary to organize the information and decide on its value in the context of each investment.

The first reason for writing this book is to step away from the tasks of day-to-day investment management and think about the investment process and the broader scope of the financial markets. Hopefully, introspection offers the opportunity to think about what data is important and what data is extraneous and answer the questions of how, when, and where the constant stream of data should be used to create superior returns. Additionally, the broader challenges facing active investment management today and how they might be affecting the execution of the investment process may be contemplated.

- What were the challenges in the 2010s?
- How will the 2020s be different?
- Why has active investing alpha declined significantly since 2010?
- How can the challenges be met?

The environment created by global central bank intervention has had many derivative effects and made active investing in the 2010s more difficult than ever; this will continue in the 2020s. Global central banks have taken center stage, capital is cheap to everyone, and momentum is a driving force in the financial markets. Refocusing on defining and executing the key investment tenets that will lead to significant outperformance is necessary to meet this challenge. Throughout this book, I define significant outperformance as averaging 1,000 basis points of alpha per year measured on a three-year rolling basis. No one can outperform every year, and the best time frame to judge an investor is five years, but a three-year rolling basis is a fair measurement. This is a lofty goal. Few managers achieve this goal and the number that do is dwindling every year. In fact, fewer and fewer managers are even getting the chance to try, because institutional allocators are moving more capital to passive investing each year.

For me, process is the key to success despite it often seeming boring and, to many who do not see the subtleties, the same. These subtleties to the investment process make a huge difference when the margin of error between under- and outperforming is so thin. Writing this book is a pursuit to further organize my own thoughts and ideas on how to optimize the investment process and understand the current environment.

You never really know something until you prepare to teach it.

My secondary career activity since 1998 has been teaching at Duke University. I taught entrepreneurship for ten years and more recently endowment investment management, a class in which many members of the Duke University management team participate. My experience in teaching has made it clear to me that organizing your thoughts to teach someone is a great learning process. No one wants to step in front of a class of young, intelligent students without being prepared, so teaching is a constant challenge to keep learning and to understand every aspect of the subject well enough to explain it to others. Trying to communicating my thought process in this book furthers my own understanding.

> *While we teach, we learn.*
>
> —*Seneca, philosopher*

I have been very fortunate to have had diverse business experiences, which have allowed me a somewhat unique perspective as an investor. Roles as an investment banking analyst, entrepreneur/CEO of a consumer business, micro/small cap hedge fund manager, and global endowment investor have progressively made my scope of business knowledge become broader and more strategic. However, my early hands-on experience running a company, selling product, and managing employees are instrumental in my daily thought process as an investor. Running and selling my company (however small in the context of the broader markets) enabled me to understand intimately many issues that play out in public companies every day. Whether it be understanding the cultural changes that occur in an acquisition, how large global brands manage their distribution channels, or the struggle to provide superior customer service to hundreds of thousands of customers every year, my operational experience colors my investing beliefs and decisions. This early decade of my career led me to a firm belief in fundamental cash flow investing and in thinking about stock ownership through the lens of a business operator.

Moving from the operational stress of running a small business dealing with thousands of individual customers daily to cofounding a micro/small cap hedge fund was my transition to being an investor. I started to define my thoughts on process and alpha creation in the earliest days of working to define our firm's *edge* for potential investors. My partner and I met with hundreds of management teams on site visits and at industry conferences. These experiences in security selection and portfolio management on both the long and short side were instrumental in the evolution of my investment process methodology. Managing the firm over a seven-year period, we enjoyed every successful investment but learned even more from each mistake. A five-year successful track record was very abruptly interrupted beginning in late 2007.

Painful errors teach you more than success does.

—*Jeremy Grantham, investor*

Managing a portfolio of micro and small cap companies through 2008 was learning at a level I hope I never get to experience again. I look back on many of my investment mistakes without much acrimony and recognize the value of the lessons learned, but the second half of 2008 was extreme. Many of our portfolio companies were down 50% by August 2008 and as our investors called capital from us to shore up their cash holdings we sold many of our micro-cap ownership positions back to the CEOs and board members in fall 2008, only to watch the stocks drop another 50% in their hands over the next few months. Trying to manage a small cap long and short portfolio during that period was an intense education in the psychological issues associated with portfolio management. We closed the firm down because too many investors were requesting capital, which led me to briefly question all the investment beliefs that had led to the firm's inception.

Fortunately (thankfully), Duke University Management Company (DUMAC) hired me to initiate their direct investing strategy. Since 2010, I have been able to further my education and refine my investment process beliefs by working with the DUMAC team and managing DUMAC's internal capital. Importantly, I have had the added benefit of learning from the strategies and thoughts of hundreds of managers that DUMAC interacts with and allocates capital to every year. The amount of human talent and research data that passes through a university endowment daily is immense and it has enabled me to evolve my thought process globally and across asset classes in ways that would not have been possible at my own hedge fund. Understanding the investment management business from both the hedge fund manager side of the table and the allocator side of the table has offered me unique insight.

This book is primarily directed at concentrated equity investment strategies with lofty goals of alpha creation. The global nature and breadth of diversification at a major endowment often call for a wide variety of investment strategies with different goals. However, the key investment tenets do not change. Understanding the ways investment methodologies can be implemented to achieve predefined risk and return goals through varying concentration levels and across different geographies and sectors has been educational.

I have interspersed quotes from well-known investors throughout the book to, I hope, add credence to many of the points. Reading their books and investment letters were, and still are, instrumental to my understanding and evolution as an investor.

Active investing is a craft that can be honed through experience and research. Of course, luck is an ever present influence in investing. Both good and bad luck influence outcomes and make learning a tricky process. The greatest tools to fight bad luck are a disciplined process and investing with the appropriate time horizon.

It has been a very tough decade for active investment managers. I hope reading this book will help everyone's results in some small way. The 2020s will be successful for those who keep learning and enhancing their investment process.

Evan L. Jones
March 2020

PART I

MARKET ENVIRONMENT: THE 2010s AND 2020s

Central bank intervention and the accelerated pace of technology are causing traditional business models to be disrupted at historic levels. Disruption is occurring across almost every industry and causes change to historic business cycles, industry power dynamics, and consumer behavior. The change is material enough to cause paradigm shifts leaving executives and investors with an unforeseeable future. These industry paradigm shifts combined with macro-driven financial markets have created one of the toughest environments for active investment managers in history.

The bolded words are present in the glossary

CHAPTER 1

CHALLENGES TO ACTIVE INVESTING

- *Active investing alpha has been falling*
- *Self-reinforcing cycle driving poor performance*
- *Why do these forces pressure investment decisions?*
- *Key investment tenets*

Creating positive **alpha** (risk-adjusted **excess return**) through active equity investing has always been hard, but it has been getting harder for today's investment managers with no clear end in sight. Spending the time and energy to investigate, analyze, and monitor companies for individual investments in the public markets takes dedication, curiosity, and experience. In the past, when done well, this work has paid off. It still can today, but the historic challenges were amplified in the 2010s and will continue in the 2020s.

The focus of Part I will be to analyze the unique challenges that arose in the 2010s for active investment managers and consider how these challenges will continue to affect the 2020s. The confluence of two separate forces has pressured the key investment tenets that have historically led to outperforming the broad equity markets. Those two forces are **massive central bank intervention** (chapter 2) and the **accelerated pace of technology** (chapter 3).

In Part II the focus will shift to an in-depth discussion of the key investment tenets and investment process necessary to outperform the public equity markets. I hope by intimately defining the keys to a successful investment process and recognizing the specific challenges in the execution of the process that managers may overcome and adapt to the challenges and produce superior returns (alpha).

Active investing alpha has been falling

Historically less than 50% of investment managers have succeeded in producing consistent long-term alpha for their clients. In recent years that number has been dwindling significantly, and overall alpha across the entire investment industry has

3

been falling. The consequence is a significant trend of capital moving from active investment strategies to **passive investment** alternatives. Passive alternatives are **exchange traded funds (ETFs)** and other similar, highly diversified factor portfolios that exactly or nearly track benchmarks. Today, allocators are questioning the value of active investment management and re-embracing many of the efficient market hypothesis beliefs developed in the 1970s. Whether it be new automated security selection technologies or factor investing designed to manage capital on a diversified risk-adjusted basis, belief in the value of fundamental active management is waning.

> *During my 87 years I have witnessed a whole succession of technological revolutions. But none of them has done away with the need for character in the individual or the ability to think.*
>
> —*Bernard Baruch, investor*

There are certainly situations in which passive investing is the best alternative. For most individual non-sophisticated investors, passive alternatives are clearly the best option. This book is geared toward professional investment managers and capital allocators interested in learning and honing the craft of active management. For this group of dedicated investment professionals alpha creation is very possible. One caveat is that alpha creation is harder in some markets than others and strategies must match expectations. Large cap investing in the US is a more difficult universe to create alpha in than small cap emerging market investing. Managers must understand both the potential and limits to their unique strategies and build their investment process on their investment goals.

There are many indices and specific methodologies by which to measure hedge fund alpha over time, and specific time periods have unique market issues, but the overall downward trend is undeniable. Figure 1.1 provides 30 years of hedge fund return data. The trend line is clear and the last decade demonstrates the pressures on the core investment tenets and decision-making that we will be discussing.

The result of the poor performance has been very poor net asset flows into hedge funds, which puts short-term pressure on hedge fund managers to perform well or risk having to close their firm. Figure 1.2 shows that it is clear that attracting capital for hedge funds has been very difficult during the 2010s. The ten years prior to the financial crisis saw a net $665 billion go into hedge funds. The financial crisis caused large outflows totaling $275 billion, which is not uncommon during times of stress. However, from 2010 to 2019, net inflows to hedge funds totaled only $105 billion. This is not only five times less than the ten-year period prior to the financial crisis but it is reclaiming less than half of the assets that were withdrawn during the crisis.

This is not an issue specific to hedge fund managers alone or an indictment of the hedge fund industry in any way. This is central to all active investment managers trying to outperform the market over the last decade. Not only has alpha been dropping, the percentage of managers who outperform at all has been dropping. Figure 1.3 demonstrates the drop in the percentage of active managers outperforming the S&P

FIGURE 1.1   36-month rolling alpha of the HFRI Fund of Funds Composite Index

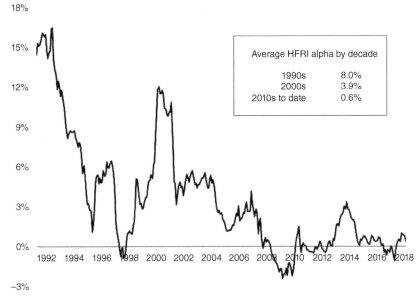

Source: Hedge Fund Research (HFR).

FIGURE 1.2   Net asset flows into hedge funds

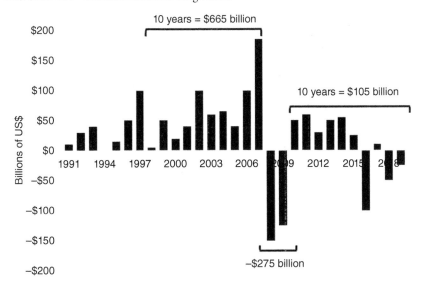

FIGURE 1.3   Percentage of US equity funds that beat the S&P 500 (five-year average)

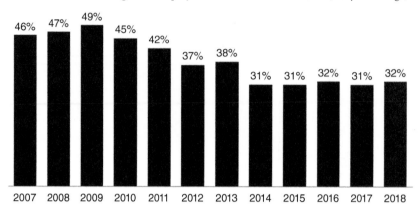

500 on a five-year average return basis. Until the 2010s the percentage of managers outperforming was in the mid-to-high 40s, but since 2010, it has dropped to the low-30s range.

The mutual fund industry is monitored separately, and the majority of mutual fund managers have underperformed their benchmarks after fees consistently for decades. In an analysis completed in June 2019 by the S&P Indices Versus Active (SPIVA) project, only 21% of large actively managed US mutual funds outperformed the S&P 500 over the previous five years. Additionally, research performed by both Vanguard and Morningstar showed 90% of large cap US mutual funds failing to outperform the S&P 500 from 2001 through 2016.

The recent market environment has not had as pronounced a negative effect on cash flows into the mutual fund industry simply because the average mutual fund manager in the 2010s focused on tracking error (**volatility** around their benchmark) and diversified away both the ability to outperform or underperform the market materially.

The challenges of the current environment will remain for a long time, and only a disciplined process designed on the core investment tenets that create outperformance will enable managers to be successful. Competent capital allocators can find alpha-producing managers to enhance their returns through a thorough due diligence process and an understanding of the alpha potential for different strategies and the pieces that need to be in place for a manager to outperform the market. Again, not an easy task, but it is achievable. Endowments, foundations, and family offices have the long-term track records demonstrating the significant value added from partnering with alpha-creating active investment managers.

In an efficient market at any point in time the actual price of a security will be a good estimate of its intrinsic value.
                        —*Eugene Fama, economics professor and Nobel laureate*

Re-embracing the beliefs of the efficient market hypothesis is understandable from an allocator's perspective when outperformance falters the way it has in the 2010s. However, the theory is often misunderstood and misused in the debate over active and passive investing. Many people define the theory as, *you can't beat the market*. Nowhere does it actually say, *no one can beat the market*. The theory put forward by Eugene Fama states there are three forms of the efficient market hypothesis (EMH): strong, semi-strong, and weak. These forms vary in strength of theoretical statement on markets being efficient and offering the potential of outperformance, but most important it is based on the concept of *average* active investment returns. There are investment managers who can and have outperformed the markets. Historically, the extent of the outperformance by investment managers is dependent on strategy (geography, sector, market cap size). Although one in five experienced managers may outperform consistently over time in the US large cap space, closer to one in two managers outperform in niche sector markets or markets outside the US. It is important to understand what an average performance will achieve, but equally important to strive and prepare to be above average.

If I subscribed to the efficient market theory I would still be delivering papers.
                                           —*Warren Buffett, investor*

Espousing the theory of efficient markets and moving capital to passive alternatives has an additional benefit to capital allocators: *job security*. No capital allocator ever underperformed the market by being in passive alternatives. From a career perspective moving to passive investing is a very low risk decision, especially when everyone else is moving the same direction. Expectations and the pressure to outperform are lower for chief investment officers if clients and fiduciaries believe that active investing cannot produce alpha. Past failures to produce alpha through active manager selection can be written off as an industry failure, not an individual capital allocation firm failure. A move to passive investing will drop expectations to a level that will always be met. No alpha expectations from clients, constituents, and board members will mean no underperformance (hence no stress) by the chief investment officer and investment team. The outcome, of course, is that they have now, also, given up any chance of outperforming.

It is very clear from my own investing and watching other active managers that outperforming the market, although difficult, is possible. Unfortunately, the 2010s were particularly difficult, and many of the best managers in the world have struggled to produce returns. Large established hedge funds have closed their doors in frustration. Efficient market theorists may point to enhanced communication via the internet, quantitative models, and fair disclosure laws as limiting factors, but there is another answer behind the recent alpha degradation.

Self-reinforcing cycle driving poor performance

The challenges created by the confluence of global central bank intervention and the accelerating pace of technology have created a negative self-reinforcing cycle for active managers The investment decision process and the core tenets of outperformance are challenged, which hurts investment returns. Poor returns drive money flows out of actively managed funds and into passive alternatives. These negative fund flows create more pressure on active investment managers to perform, which drives short-term decision making. Of course, short-term focus and chasing returns leads to more poor performance and more flows into passive alternatives. Once started, this is a tough cycle to stop.

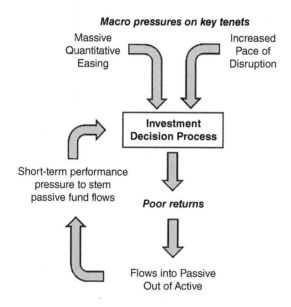

Why do these forces pressure investment decisions?

Massive central bank intervention creates a market driven by macro issues. The focus is on central bank statements and interviews of bureaucrats on how they foresee the next six months. Central bank–driven low rates push all investors into riskier assets, because traditional low-risk investment alternatives provide uncompelling returns. When capital allocators cannot achieve their defined investment return goals due to low bond yields, they have little choice but to take on more **risk** in the form of higher equity exposure to achieve objectives. This demand for equity and risk capital creates high valuations and enables weak companies to flourish. Allocators believe the central banks will act as support to markets making the additional risk more palatable. The central banks try to fulfill the need for low volatility and market stability for the good of the markets and the economy. Another dangerous cycle is created as global central banks manipulate investors into pushing asset prices higher to spur the economy, but in doing so have increased the risk profile of the investment community, which, of course, could lead to potential losses negatively affecting the economy. This means central banks must go to even greater lengths to maintain low levels of volatility and support the financial markets. Easy access to capital, low rates, and low volatility cause another headwind for hedge fund managers, which is the dispersion of stock returns among companies. Good companies and bad companies alike do well in upward-trending macro-driven markets. Successful investment managers achieve outperformance by selecting the strong companies and shorting the weak companies. When there is very little difference in returns, it is hard to create alpha. An analysis produced by the BoA Merrill Lynch Quantitative Strategy team in Figure 1.4 illustrates the level of dispersion in the returns of the top-performing quintile and bottom-performing quintile of stocks in the S&P 500. High dispersion is a positive environment for alpha creation, because there are more distinct winners and losers for a manager to choose in the security selection process. Low dispersion (more stocks moving in unison) is a headwind to alpha creation. It is clear from the analysis that dispersion has been below average since 2010, when central bank intervention began.

FIGURE 1.4   S&P 500 dispersion of the top and bottom decile from 1986 to June 2019

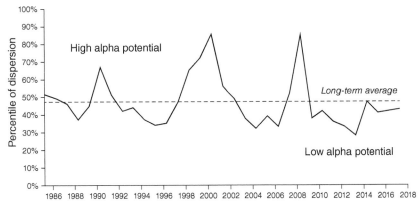

Source: Adapted from BoA Merrill Lynch US Equity & Quantitative Strategy Group (August 2019).

The central bank low rate–driven environment pushes investors into risk assets, which often equates to investment in high-growth, no-earnings companies. This increased willingness to invest in companies without earnings amplifies the already accelerating pace of technology. Combined the two forces of easy money and an increased pace of technology innovation create disruption in industries and a major challenge to the core investment tenets that have driven outperformance historically. The following diagram illustrates the different ways high demand for risk assets affect active investment manager decisions creating headwinds for alpha creation. To be clear, this artificially driven demand for risk assets is not all bad for society or the economy. It does create the potential for financial bubbles, which can be problematic.

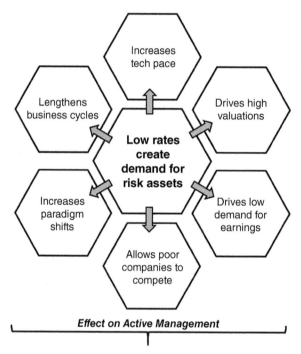

We will dig deeper into central bank intervention and the accelerated pace of technology in chapters 2 and 3, but first we need to briefly introduce the key investment tenets that are coming under magnified pressure. Although there is no one right way to be a successful active investment manager, the following investment tenets, to be developed fully in Part II, are central to the majority of successful fundamentally based equity investment firms.

Key investment tenets

In order to discuss the unique challenges of today's environment in relation to history, it is worth quickly defining the key investment tenets in question.

Goal congruence and fiduciary responsibility

This is the investment tenet that will never change. Very simply, if you do not have **goal congruence** in an investment or with an investment manager nothing else matters. If a management team or investment manager causes you to question his or her integrity as a fiduciary of your capital, you should investigate your concerns, and if they are not completely alleviated simply move onto other opportunities. The rest of the investment decision process means nothing without trust in the people and numbers you are analyzing. The great thing about the investment industry, in general, is that there are many, many opportunities.

Invest in business fundamentals

Unlike the simplicity of being a good fiduciary, fundamental analysis and security selection is a very long, detailed, and nuanced subject. The amount of work and difficulty in understanding the many important facets of a business cause many investors to take shortcuts. These shortcuts can often have the eventual effect that the business fundamentals themselves are forgotten. Decisions begin to be made based on the *stock* and its price actions, not on the business and its fundamental cash flow creation. Fundamental business analysis with an emphasis on future cash flow creation and growth involves an extensive list of issues related to industry dynamics, market growth, competition, capital allocation, cost structure, management, and more.

Understand the role of valuation in future returns

Understand the business and its future potential, but then understand the effect of the point in time that your investment is made and the valuation you choose to pay. An investor's valuation entry point and future additions and sales of the investment are paramount to the final return outcome. I have avoided the term *value investing*, because it can be defined by some as buying cheap stocks, which is simplistic and will not create superior returns (although it is better than simplistically buying expensive stocks). Part II will develop how to think about the predictive power of valuation and the importance of multiples and cash flow yields in creating superior returns.

Contrarianism

Superior returns are generally created by being a contrarian and finding opportunities where the market has punished good companies, sectors, or countries and you can see a different future. If you are correct in recognizing a future successful company, that is a stock market darling today and trading at very high equity valuations, you will only return the beta-adjusted cost of equity capital. We will look at some specific and subtle issues concerning contrarianism. Being a contrarian in today's market environment is harder than ever before.

> *Prices fluctuate more than values—so therein lies opportunity.*
> —*Joel Greenblatt, investor*

Time horizon

Fundamental investing and contrarianism take time. You have to be afforded the time to allow your thesis to play out. In many instances, the markets do not accurately reflect the value of a company's future cash flows at a certain point in time due to exogenous factors. This is wonderful for good investors, and one of the primary reasons outperforming the market is possible, but it means you have to have the time to allow the market to correct and your thesis to play out. If you are forced to be a short-term investor, a huge advantage in your ability to outperform has been lost.

Portfolio concentration

Analyzing companies and making good individual investment decisions can be very different than being a good portfolio manager. Understanding how to construct a portfolio to offer the opportunity to outperform, yet managing risk, is both quantitative and qualitative. Liquidity and volatility can be quantitatively measured, but an understanding of the real-life implications of those numbers and how it will affect your decision-making is experiential. Portfolio concentration, making significant investments as a percentage of your capital, is necessary to create alpha. The level of concentration is dependent on the alpha and volatility goals of the firm. The challenges of managing a concentrated portfolio are not dissimilar from the pre-financial crisis period, but again they are magnified due to the amplified role of global central banks and technologically driven disruption. In the 2010s, macro issues have overwhelmed individual company decisions, and risks not generally associated with an individual company have often dictated short-term performance.

Behavioral pitfalls

Understanding the behavioral mistakes that affect every manager is the first step in overcoming (or limiting) those mistakes. Selling winners too early, letting the market rule your emotions, and trading too much are only a few of the pitfalls that must be overcome through experience and analysis. Behavioral mistakes in portfolio management are one of the top reasons, if not the top reason, investment managers fail to outperform the market. The magnification of both the potential for down-side risk and FOMO (fear of missing out) create pressure on the behavioral control necessary to be successful.

> *I must take care not to compound my error by reacting emotionally. I must adapt to changing circumstances.*
>
> —*George Soros, investor*

Process

Investment process is both the key to long-term development as an investor and to creating a firm that can grow without dependence on one individual. Success in the investment management industry is very hard to come by, but even harder to replicate. How can you replicate something that has so many different variables and potential outcomes?

Active investing is a discipline in which being 70% correct is a great track record and in which you can be wrong for the right reasons and right for the wrong reasons. A strategy can look horrible today only to look brilliant a year in the future. The only chance an investor has to honestly judge actions and learn from mistakes and success is to painstakingly create a process of investing that incorporates both security selection and portfolio management. A large part of this process is documentation in the form of an original investment thesis and then regular updates on events that affect the thesis.

To make it even more difficult your process cannot be 100% rigid and static. There are too many unique scenarios, and every investor continues to learn and markets change. The core investment tenets we are discussing may not change, but any completely static process is not growing and evolving. We will discuss where to draw the line between a process that can evolve and become better over time, as opposed to one that is ever-changing and has no foundation.

My conviction in the core investment tenets described not only comes from 20 years of portfolio management experience but also from the opportunity to watch and interact with some of the world's best managers. The investment business is somewhat unusual in that understanding which decision was an error, even in hindsight, is not always readily apparent. It is possible to make the right decision and have a poor result. It is, also, possible to make the wrong decision and be handsomely paid. Some might not call being handsomely paid a wrong decision, but it may be a decision that nine times out of ten will cost you money; you just happened to be lucky in the timing of the investment.

Which experiences are beneficial lessons and which are red herrings?

Individual investment managers do not get the opportunity to analyze a huge dataset of decisions, because there may only be a handful of major decisions made each year.

The conclusions take time to become clear. Major periods of market stress are not very frequent, so the dataset of events to learn from is not large. For this reason, I am very appreciative of having learned not just from my own mistakes but also from watching and talking to the hundreds of global managers that DUMAC has partnered with in the 2010s. My dataset of decisions to analyze and consider has been 100 times what it would have been if I were to have solely managed my own fund and been confined to my experiences.

The next two chapters delve into more detail on the current market environment and the two forces challenging investment decisions today: central bank intervention and technology-driven disruption.

CHAPTER 2

GLOBAL CENTRAL BANK INTERVENTION

- *Unprecedented global central bank intervention*
- *Fundamental investing overwhelmed by central bank intervention*
- *Low rates and the US consumer*

Unprecedented global central bank intervention

Global central bank policy after the 2008 financial crisis and the 2011 euro crisis has been analyzed in hundreds of books and by brilliant economists. The focus here is not on whether it was the right thing to do or could have been done better but on the effect quantitative easing and low rates has had on companies and investment managers' ability to outperform the market.

Global central banks have been actively involved in fueling the developed world economies (US, Europe, and Japan) for the past decade at a level that has never been seen before in history. The Federal Reserve (Fed), European Central Bank (ECB), and Bank of Japan (BoJ) have not worked in exact coordination, but they have followed similar paths. The effect has been that global central banks have been the number one driver of equity markets. The age-old maxim "Don't fight the Fed" has never been more apt than in recent history. US Federal Reserve governors are the new investment rock stars driving financial valuations to historic highs in the 2010s. Central banks globally have succeeded in lowering rates, ensuring credit accessibility, and raising the value of all financial assets without growth in inflation to date. Figure 2.1 depicts the growth in central bank assets of each of the three major developed world central banks in trillions of US dollars.

The magnitude of the asset growth is over 300% since 2007, and globally central banks have purchased over $15 trillion in assets, while GDP growth around the world has been stagnate. Each time one of the central banks has tried to ease off there has been a recessionary scare and they have jumped back in to support a fragile global economy. You can see by the solid line that the US has tried since 2015 to wean

FIGURE 2.1   Global central bank assets—US Fed, Bank of Japan, and European Central Bank (2002 to November 2019)

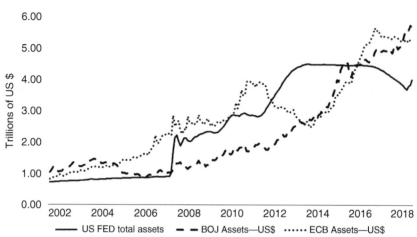

itself off the Federal Reserve support system, but as of the fourth quarter of 2019 slow growth and low inflation has the Federal Reserve once again supporting the markets with expected rate cuts and an increase in assets. Back in 2008, no one would have predicted that ten years after the 2008 financial crisis global central banks would hold this level of assets.

Europe and Japan have not even attempted to slow levels of monetary support. Sovereign rates in these countries have been pushed into negative territory through the magnitude of central bank intervention, a feat that most investors and academics never thought could happen. In November 2019, an investor expected to *pay* the German government 0.35% and the Japanese government 0.15% to lend the government money for ten years. The ECB holds close to 20% of the sovereign debt of EU countries and has been buying as much as 90% of new issuance in certain months. Paying to lend a country money (buying sovereign bonds) or anyone for that matter does not make economic sense and blows up traditional quantitative models and risk analyses; yet is becoming a normal occurrence in developed world sovereign markets.

The Bank of Japan holds over 50% of all Japan sovereign debt outstanding and has led the quantitative easing experiment by also buying corporate bonds and equity ETFs. The BoJ began buying equity ETFs in 2010 to support the country's equity markets after the financial crisis. It continues to support the equity markets ten years later. In the years 2017, 2018, and 2019 the Japanese central bank bought an average of $50 billion of Japanese equity ETFs each year in an attempt to support the country's equity markets. In 2018, the balance sheet of the BoJ surpassed the country's GDP. The BoJ holds over $5 trillion in Japanese financial assets. The buying is not only unprecedented but also not sustainable.

Central banks would like to raise rates and return to some semblance of a normal rate environment, but they are up against two forces that are proving difficult. Inflation has been below normal levels despite zero percent rates, high asset prices, and large amounts of liquidity and capital in the economy. Globalization provided cheap labor and a large portion of the manufacturing base in the US and Europe moved overseas in the new century. This trend lowered prices and had a dampening effect on inflation. By 2015, the globalization trend had matured, but technology and demographics are now acting as key inflation-dampening forces. The US and Europe are debtor nations, and inflating away debt is the easiest and most comfortable path for debtors. Deflation would be a major problem for both government and consumer debt obligations. The Federal Reserve and all global central banks are very aware of the perils of deflation and the need for inflation. Even if the economy is growing nicely and unemployment levels are low, it would be difficult for central banks to return to historic interest rate levels, if inflation were not to move above 2.0%

> *History is inflationary; governments promise more than they can provide and they never want voters' assets to be worth less than before.*
>
> —*Will Durant, historian*

Unfortunately, developed economies are not growing at historic rates, if at all. This is another key driver that keeps central banks from raising rates. Neither Europe nor Japan is showing enough growth to even consider lowering support. Eurozone GDP growth has not hit 2.5% since before 2010 and future expectations are anemic at 1% to 2%. Japan has been even worse despite larger levels of support from the Bank of Japan. Growth rates in the developed world as a whole have been below 2% on average since 2010 and are forecasted to stay at these historically low levels.

So a lack of growth and inflation despite historically high levels of asset buying and low rates keeps the central banks from raising rates. Interest rates have remained below 2% globally with Europe and Japan rates below zero. Any time investors perceive rates to be rising they flee the markets and growth slows even further forcing global banks to reconsider any rate raises. This is a rate environment that was never anticipated, especially with US unemployment levels below 4% and the US stock market reaching all-time highs (3,100+ on the S&P 500 in November 2019). There is no historic data on this level of central bank intervention, so derivative effects are not known in the intermediate or long term. Despite (or because of) this, equity and bond markets remain unperturbed, demonstrating the lowest volatility levels in history. The 2010s will be remembered for central bank intervention driving the lowest rates in history and the equity markets demonstrating the lowest levels of volatility.

> *[On 0% interest rates] I can't figure out how it's going to end. I just know it's going to end badly.*
>
> —*Stanley Druckenmiller, investor*

Can central banks unwind their asset purchases over the next decade?

A complete unwind or a return to central bank asset levels pre-2008 will either never take place or at least not occur for decades. There is no way that the Fed, ECB, and BOJ can sell a majority of their assets back into the market in any intermediate time frame.

> *[In July 2014] I hope we can all agree that once-in-a-century emergency measures are no longer necessary five years into an economic recovery.*
>
> —*Stanley Druckenmiller, investor*

Not unwinding the central bank asset growth does not mean rates will always be close to zero, but historical interest rate levels will not be seen for many years. Looking at the 20-year history of the Federal Funds rate in Figure 2.2, rates have been 4%, 5%, and even 6% at certain periods. A Federal Funds rate at 5% is impossible to imagine today. The hope central bankers hold is that a small amount of growth in GDP and inflation over many years, while holding assets flat, can right size their balance sheet. Federal Reserve increases in 2016 and 2017 were quickly reversed as the economy demonstrated its fragility and capital markets started to drop.

If the central banks can simply maintain assets at $15 trillion, potentially the developed world economies can grow (and inflate) into a scenario where $15 trillion does not look that extreme. It is a delicately balanced scale. Investors have remained confident and taken on more risk, and to date the US Federal Reserve has maintained continual support of the markets.

Inflating the value of financial assets has been the one goal that the Fed has been able to master. Low rates and promises to promote growth at any cost has supported financial markets and consumer confidence in general, but it has had a

FIGURE 2.2   US Federal Funds rate (1998 to November 2019)

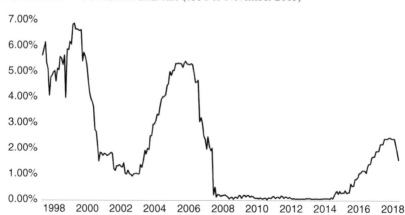

FIGURE 2.3   Federal Reserve assets and the S&P 500 Index (2001 to November 2019)

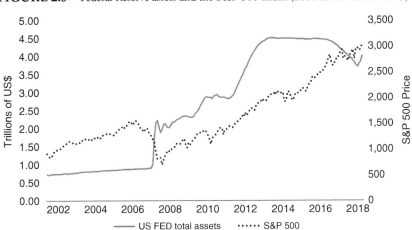

derivative effect. Financial asset growth has created the greatest wealth divide since the 1920s. If you own financial assets, you are prosperous and if you do not own financial assets you have been left behind. Figure 2.3 shows a graph of the S&P 500 and the Federal Reserve assets since 2001. It would be hard to dispute the causation of Fed intervention and equity performance. The Fed tried to raise rates in 2017 and 2018, because unemployment dropped below 5% and the economy seemed to be expanding, but the equity markets stalled, scaring the Fed into cutting rates once again in 2019 and renewing asset growth.

Fundamental investing overwhelmed by central bank intervention

For a fundamental investment manager this is evidence that macro news and events are driving markets, not fundamental business results. In the 2020s, the markets can progress down two different paths. The first is a continuation of the 2010s, which will be a struggle for active investing, as we have discussed. The second path would be more ominous, as investors lose confidence in central banks. There seems to be little indication that a third option of growth and normalcy will arise. The path of global economies rebounding significantly allowing central banks to stop their intervention has little supportive data. Central banks have taken on the incredible responsibility of stabilizing and supporting financial markets for the next decade.

A macro-driven market, as the Fed has created through constant intervention, takes the emphasis away from fundamental investing. At the core of any investment strategy that outperforms the market is investing based on future expectations of cash flows produced by a company. A security selection thesis can be articulated by managers in many different ways. Investing in a business may be based on operating margin growth, entering new markets, facing weaker competition, creating a technological advantage, or having an elite management team, but they equate to expecting stronger cash flows in the future than the market expects today. Central bank intervention has materially lowered the relationship of fundamental company security selection and equity performance. Multiples are more volatile than earnings, so if multiples are going to be driven by outside factors, cash flows will have less explanatory effect.

> *[In January 2015] Earnings don't move the overall market, it's the Federal Reserve Board... Focus on the central banks and focus on the movement of liquidity... It's liquidity that moves markets.*
>
> —*Stanley Druckenmiller, investor*

Diligently studying a company's operations to understand future growth does not add the same value to future equity performance when a central bank dictates the markets and low rates make all stocks go up due to higher valuation multiples. An additional driver of valuation multiples today is technological disruption. Certain sectors of the S&P 500 have been decimated by actual or perceived future disruption and are trading at historically low multiples balancing the historically high multiples of other rate-sensitive sectors. Retailers' valuations have been destroyed by Amazon's success, energy producers have been destroyed by supply gluts created by fracking disruption, and health care services trade at all-time lows due to regulation concerns and technology company threats to the established industry leaders. This confluence of cheap, easy money and disruption is the challenge pressuring active managers. If we focus on S&P 500 sectors that are rate sensitive and have not seen large-scale technological disruption, we can see the massive effect on valuations from low rates.

> *When capital is in oversupply, investors compete for deals by accepting low returns and a slender margin for error.*
>
> —*Howard Marks, investor*

Utilities are one of the most rate-sensitive sectors and to date have not been negatively influenced by technological disruption. Figure 2.4 shows price-to-earnings (P/E) multiples in the 2010s. Multiples have grown over 60%. Utilities are historically a cost of capital return sector, where very few investment managers spend much time due to the slow-paced, regulation-influenced business model. Low rates have made it a top-performing sector.

During the same time frame that P/E ratios rose, utilities had incredibly easy access to capital at very low rates due to investor demand for their debt. From 2010 to 2019, the S&P 500 utilities sector created negative-free cash flow every year and increased dividends every year. Figure 2.5 illustrates the upward dividend per share trend and

FIGURE 2.4   S&P 500 utilities sector trailing 12-month P/E ratio (2009 to November 2019)

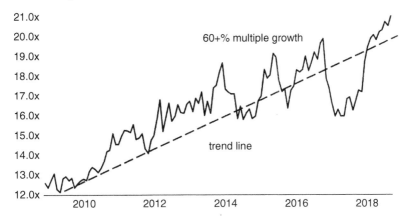

FIGURE 2.5   S&P 500 utilities sector dividends paid per share and free cash flow per share (2009 to November 2019)

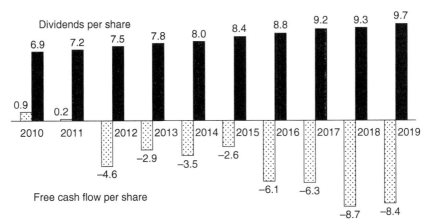

the downward free cash flow trend. All dividends during the last decade were paid for with newly issued debt. The sector now trades at a net debt to cash flow ratio of 6.7 times. This is the highest level of net debt in history, completely supported by low rates and a chase for yield by investors. Utilities are a very stable industry historically, but any disruption caused by renewables and consumers' ability to generate electricity independently to move off the grid will cause a severe down trend given the sector's debt levels.

Another rate-sensitive sector driven by margin stability and large established brand-focused business model is the consumer staples sector. Again, technological disruption has not had a huge influence on the sector (yet) and the sector has been primarily influenced by low rates driven by the Fed (and in Europe by the ECB). Investors have bought into the sector as a *bond proxy*. When bond rates drop to levels that will not provide the necessary return to an institutional investor, there is a move out the risk curve in a search for yield. Investors have decided that the consumer staples sector is an equity safe haven. Figure 2.6 illustrates the significant multiple expansion that has occurred in the sector, as investors pay up to own consumer staples. In a low-rate environment, investors who may generally hold 30% or 40% of their capital in Treasuries or investment-grade corporate bonds must either accept lower returns than they have achieved historically or take on more risk.

If an institutional investment mandate is to achieve 5%–6% real (after inflation) returns and the ten-year Treasury trades at 2.5% with inflation at 2.0% (yielding a 0.5% real return), what are your options?

The first would be to maintain traditional capital-allocation exposures and convince constituents that they should accept lower returns (not usually a readily accepted path). The second would be to sell bonds and buy riskier assets, usually equities. Because allocators know they have taken on more risk in selling safer bonds, they will search for lower risk equity solutions, like utilities, consumer staples, and minimum volatility–factor ETFs, all of which have very extended multiples. These rate-driven investor decisions and valuation increases have nothing to do with fundamental investing and pressure the success of any active manager. Macro concerns and Fed decisions overwhelm business analysis.

FIGURE 2.6   S&P 500 consumer staples sector trailing 12-month P/E ratio (2009 to November 2019)

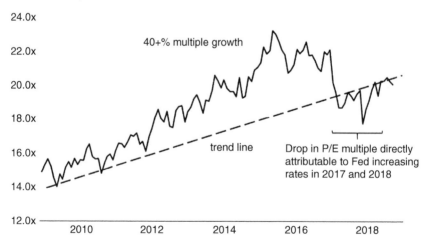

Some may point to the overall S&P 500 P/E multiple as being in line with historic levels, but that does not tell the entire story. Price is only half of the P/E equation. Revenues and earnings (operating margins) have also been pushed to historic highs by low rates. Net income margins have been heavily influenced by lower interest expense, lower commodity costs, and lower wage inflation. Of course, the Trump administration's 2017 corporate tax reform lowered tax rates and drove net margin growth even further. Looking at the 30-year S&P 500 net income margin in Figure 2.7, you can see that net margins are at or near their 30-year highs. This coincides with the longest expansion in history, now ten years long. Most long-term successful investment managers create a great deal of their outperformance in down markets when security selection driven by strong balance sheets, barriers to entry, and a deep understanding of their businesses can make a major difference. These fundamental issues that become apparent in a down market have not been an important driver of returns for a decade.

The fact is almost anyone can achieve positive absolute returns in a trending up market. Watch TV and listen to market pundits, buy the hot stocks of the day, and ignore valuation. Growth and **momentum** have been the lessons learned by new portfolio managers in the 2010s.

Only when the tide goes out, do you discover who has been swimming naked.
—Warren Buffett

When the tide goes out, good investors create outperformance. Global central banks have made sure the tide has not gone out for a decade. US equity market drawdowns of more than 10% have occurred only four times in the last decade and each drawdown has lasted less than 60 days.

FIGURE 2.7   S&P 500 net income margin (1990 to November 2019)

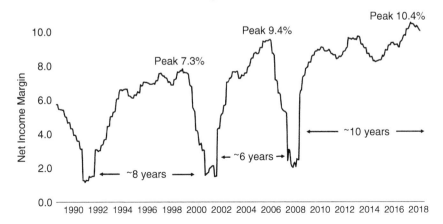

FIGURE 2.8   S&P 500 price-to-sales ratio (1990 to November 2019)

Price-to-sales ratio is a good valuation metric to review when thinking about markets from a top-down holistic perspective. High operating margins are evidenced in the multiple more so than other valuation methodologies. You can see in Figure 2.8 that we have surpassed the dot-com era valuation levels using this valuation metric. This combination of net income margin and valuation multiple expansion has created an environment in which even a historically mild recession will cause a large equity market drawdown.

Low rates have also allowed weaker companies to prosper due to the cheap and easily available credit environment. This scenario of high valuations and weak companies prospering creates the worst environment for fundamental investors to create excess returns.

Low rates and the US consumer

If inflating assets was the primary success of central bank intervention, creating a low rate environment to support US consumer spending was the second success. Federal Reserve support has kept the US consumer happy with low rates and flush with credit. Consumer purchases are made with either current income or credit. Current income has not grown and can be driven only by a thriving economy and even then income only grows marginally each year. Credit can be greatly influenced by low rates and new financing strategies. Credit growth has been the primary driver behind the US consumer economy for more than 30 years, but low rates have had a material influence since the 2008 financial crisis. Consumer spending now drives the entire US economy, because US manufacturing strength has waned since the 1990s. Consumer-related companies, regardless of their quality, competitive positioning, or good management, are strengthened by cheap, easy consumer credit.

When consumers spend at the levels they have over the last decade, it covers up a lot of operating or capital allocation mistakes made by subpar consumer companies. The success of subpar companies hurts the security selection differentiation contribution to investment alpha. If credit were to slow or rates rise, the weaker companies would falter and good research would be rewarded.

Mortgage rates have been maintained in the 4.0% range for ten years, saving the consumer thousands of dollars a year on mortgage interest. Home buyers generally do not really care what they pay for a house; what they care about is whether they can afford the monthly payment. A $300,000 home purchased with a 90% loan to value mortgage at 4% rather than 7% will save the homeowner about $9,000 per year. Another way to think about mortgage rates and home values is that for every 1% (100 **basis points**) drop in the mortgage rate a homeowner can pay about $50,000 more for the same house. That same homeowner who bought a $300,000 home at 7% can afford a $450,000 home at 4% mortgage rates. This is both a boost to housing prices and to consumer sentiment and spurs a willingness to borrow and spend. Figure 2.9 illustrates the downward trend in mortgage rates since 1997.

Auto loans, student loans, and credit card debt are the other keys to a confident, spending consumer. Figure 2.10 shows outstanding US credit card debt in millions of dollars. Low rates have created the ability to take on more credit card debt by consumers and the willingness for financial institutions to take more risk. Credit card debt outstanding has increased 300% since the 1990s. Figure 2.10 highlights the huge increase in outstanding credit card debt over both the last decade and the prior decade.

There was a time when consumers routinely paid cash for automobiles, then three-year auto loans were extended to five years to spur sales by lowering monthly payments. Today seven-year loans are very common and zero percent financing is a

FIGURE 2.9   30-year average US fixed mortgage rate (1997 to November 2019)

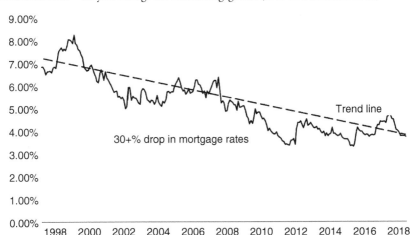

FIGURE 2.10   US outstanding credit card debt (1997 to October 2019)

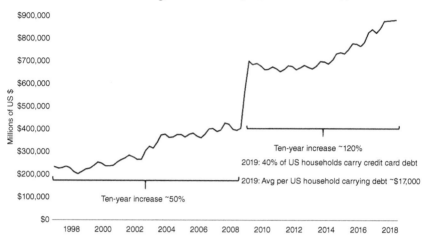

common selling point for auto companies that have created financing subsidiaries that would not exist if the markets were not willing to take risk in a search for yield. Student loans have delinquency rates over 50% and many students expect (hope) their loans will simply be forgiven by the government, which given the importance of consumer spending and avoiding deflation may be a likely outcome.

In total, the average US consumer has benefitted by approximately $1,000 per month since the 2008 financial crisis due to low rates and easy credit access. This is massive stimulus considering the average median income in the US is approximately $60,000 and has barely risen this decade. An increase of $1,000 after tax per month is more than a 25% after-tax income increase for the median household. If mortgage, auto loan, and credit card rates were to increase back to historical levels, consumer spending would drop precipitously causing significant problems for the overall economy.

The increased after-tax income has been spent in the 2010s driving the S&P 500 consumer discretionary sector up over 400%, as seen in figure 2.11. This gain includes the many retailers that have been disrupted due to e-commerce competition. If there had been any recession or consumer spending slowdown during the last ten years, dozens of additional retail chains would have closed their doors. In the 2020s decade, there will be many more retail store closings, as both disruption and a slower economy combine to add stress to the retail industry.

Americans have been the beneficiaries of all this credit through increased consumption. From the perspective of an investment manager all consumer-related companies have been major beneficiaries and have had success beyond historical standards. This, again, lowers the contribution of security selection due to their being little benefit in avoiding weaker companies. Going forward, any changes in

FIGURE 2.11   S&P 500 Consumer Discretionary Sector Price Index (2009 to October 2019)

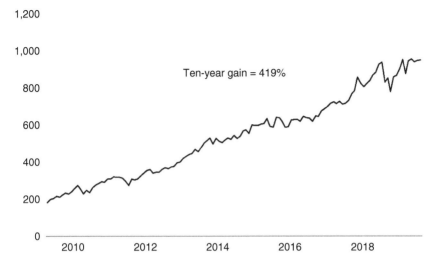

the cost or accessibility of consumer credit should be closely monitored by investors. Low rates and credit accessibility have pulled consumer demand forward, as buyers take advantage of cheap credit opportunities. At some point in time, there will be a contraction in credit accessibility or consumers will become more concerned about their future earnings potential and consumer spending will slow from these historically high levels.

The US consumer has been the most resilient part of the American economy in the 2010s buoyed by the central bank–driven low rates and credit accessibility. As evidenced in the University of Michigan Consumer Sentiment Index (Figure 2.12),

FIGURE 2.12   University of Michigan Consumer Sentiment Index (1994 to October 2019)

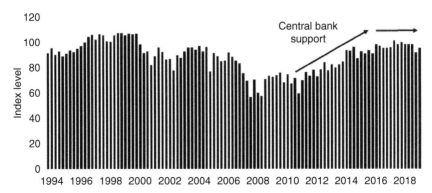

sentiment rose from 2010 to 2016 and has now plateaued. Sentiment is cyclical and does not generally last for more than a decade. Eventually consumer sentiment and demand weaken. Consumer companies will face slowing revenues, increasing margins, and industry disruption after a decade of strong consumer spending and cost savings driven by the globalization of supply chains.

The power and breadth of low rates has clearly been the most important driver of financial markets in the 2010s, but technological disruption is a close second, and there is a synergistic relationship between the two most prominent forces of the 2010s.

CHAPTER 3

ACCELERATED PACE OF TECHNOLOGY = DISRUPTION

- *Innovation adoption tipping point*
- *Innovation and financial capital*
- *Outperformance potential with unprofitable but disruptive companies?*
- *Private markets overheating?*
- *Contrarianism and paradigm shifts*

Capitalism has always been about change and disruption. Joseph Schumpeter, the well-known Austrian economist, formulated his theories on innovation and capitalism back in the early 1900s. Popularizing the term *creative destruction,* Schumpeter conceptually described the path of innovation and its effect on the economy, specifically economic growth. Innovation comes in waves or cycles with every major innovation producing disequilibrium in the economy. At the same time, innovation creates new opportunities as new businesses are born and older business models are disrupted. As one innovation goes from idea to production to early adopter to mass use, the original innovation spurs new ideas and they develop on their own life cycle, eventually sending the original innovation into decline. There is a continual process of human innovation spurred by a capitalistic system that rewards innovation due to the ability to make money. This process of creative destruction has been occurring for decades and is generally positive for society.

> *At the heart of capitalism is creative destruction.*
>
> —*Joseph A. Schumpeter, economist*

The question for investment managers is,

Why is the faster pace of creative destruction more important to active investing today?

What Schumpeter could not have had much insight into was how these waves of innovation would change in length of cycle and the amplification of their effect on economic development and disruption. There are two major factors that determine the speed of new innovation and their speed to mass use: technology and capital.

Many leaders in the technology field believe the nature of recent technologies themselves are shortening the length of innovation cycles. New technologies and discoveries are building on themselves to quicken the pace of innovation and adoption. Gordon Moore of Intel formed the hypothesis that the number of transistors in an integrated circuit would double every two years, and this theory has held in the electronic circuit industry. It may not hold for all technological innovation, but the core of the idea is that technology compounds on itself, and whether it will double every two years or four years, there is an amplification process.

> *At least 40% of all businesses will die in the next ten years … if they don't figure*
> *out how to change their entire company to accommodate new technologies.*
> *—John Chambers, Cisco Systems*

Figure 3.1 provides a simple chart demonstrating recent innovations and each innovations' time in years to adoption by 25% of the US population. In an analysis done by Ray Kurzwell, the famed futurist, it took 46 years for 25% of the US population to have electricity in their homes, 26 years to put a television in 25% of US homes, and 7 years to get 25% of US homes on the web. The speed of adoption is clearly accelerating. The tipping point for investors is that the time of adoption is now within one business cycle. Disruption and **paradigm shifts** occurring faster

FIGURE 3.1   Innovation adoption: Number of years to 25% US population adoption

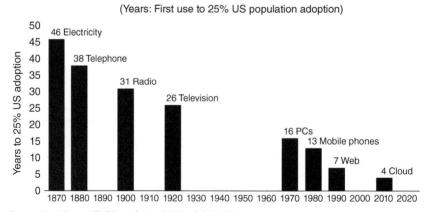

Source: Ray Kurzwell, "Singularity Is Near" (2005).

than business cycles leave investing with a contrarian or mean reverting thesis open to large losses. When there is a higher probability that an industry is being disrupted, reversion to normal is less likely to happen.

Innovation adoption tipping point

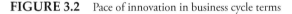

For fundamental investors, this quickening pace of disruption is problematic. As the model in Figure 3.2 conceptually demonstrates, innovation has driven the speed of adoption and therefore disruption. In the 1940s, innovation-driven change took on average 28 years, which is the span of four average economic cycles. In the 1990s, innovation change took on average 14 years, or two economic cycles. Today innovation-driven change takes less than seven years to disrupt an industry. Disruption within that time period, the average length of a historical business cycle, opens investors to the higher probability that their cyclical investment will actually be a paradigm shift.

Faster paradigm shifts call into question all mean reversion–based strategies in a way they never were before. This is very evident in deep value-based mean-reversion strategies, but any strategy that has an underlying assumption that we return to a prior status quo in the next economic cycle is under pressure.

Investors for decades have generally been able to rely on which sectors will outperform during different stages of an economic cycle. The difficulty in achieving your expected return revolved around being correct on time horizon, avoiding excess **leverage** that might bankrupt the company before the next cycle upturn, and managing the position well through market volatility (avoiding behavioral mistakes).

FIGURE 3.2   Pace of innovation in business cycle terms

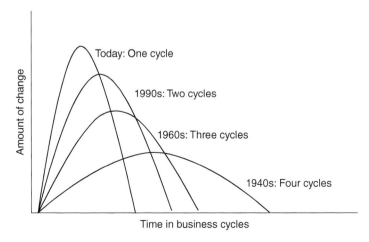

These are not simple challenges, and only a minority of managers progressed through these challenges with positive alpha. However, the biggest risk to mean reversion investments and contrarian investments is a paradigm shift. There is no mean reversion if the industry changes.

> *As a value manager you live in dread of a paradigm shift—something changes and leaves you high and dry forever.*
>
> —*Jeremy Grantham, investor*

Although Figure 3.3 is overly simplistic, mean reversion is the primary theory for a number of multibillion-dollar investment management firms. Investors may have very complex strategies and mountains of research and data backing up their strategy, but often strategies boil down to a few core investment beliefs, and mean reversion is one of them. This confluence of capital and disruption has had a significant effect on the concept of mean reversion and must be recognized by investors.

To further pressure mean reversion strategies, the economic cycle has been extended longer than ever before (as we surpass ten years), and the cycle of disruption (paradigm shifts) has shortened significantly. This one change alone will hurt many active investment manager returns significantly.

FIGURE 3.3   Economic cycles and mean reversion

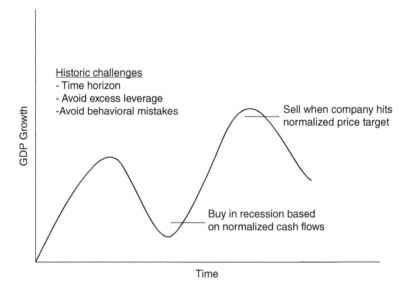

Innovation and Financial Capital

The second major factor in driving innovation is risk capital. Entrepreneurs and researchers can move only as quickly as access to capital allows them to take losses. By definition, early innovation is not profit producing and needs development and growth capital. Access to risk capital driven by investors' appetite for risk is the number one factor in the pace of innovation. Whether that innovation be a start-up in Silicon Valley or new projects at Amazon and Google, the appetite for risk capital by investors is a determining factor.

This is where the confluence of central bank intervention and the accelerated pace of technology compound to dramatically increase disruption. Almost every industry is being disrupted in some fashion, and companies no longer stay within their industry verticals. Google is disrupting industries from autos to medical devices. Amazon is no longer just threatening retail but has moved into everything from health care to cloud computing. The competitive environment can no longer be narrowly defined by industry. This would not be possible if investors were demanding earnings. It would not be possible if money were not moving aggressively into private equity, and it would not be possible if interest rates were 400 basis points higher than they are today.

Venture capital is the clearest indicator of investor willingness to finance innovation and accept losses in a quest for growth. More US venture capital has been invested in the last five years than the previous ten years combined. Figure 3.4 illustrates venture capital investing since 2004 and the huge growth in the last five years. Pre–2008 financial crisis investing levels that were considered high at the time have been surpassed every year post–financial crisis.

FIGURE 3.4   US venture capital invested by deal flow (billions of $US)

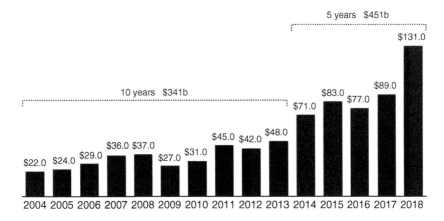

FIGURE 3.5   US share of global venture capital

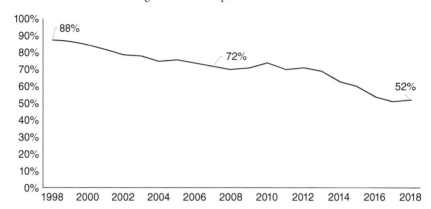

This is not solely a US phenomenon. Venture capital outside the US has been grow-ing even faster. As evidenced in Figure 3.5, the US now accounts for about 52% of global venture capital assets, whereas China and the rest of the world (RoW) split the remaining share. The US dominated venture capital for decades and even as recently as 2012 held 70% of the global share. A focus on education in science, technology, and engineering throughout the emerging world, especially China and India, has spurred innovation. Venture capital has followed the human capital to India and China. India and China both now have the human capital and growth potential to support a thriv-ing venture capital community. For decades, the US has innovated and designed, and the rest of the world has copied and produced. The 2020s will start to see that US innovation advantage be diluted.

The other significant change is that venture capitalists are no longer seeding just start-ups and emerging companies and racing to bring them public or sell them. They are holding companies privately longer than ever before allowing them to oper-ate in a non-earnings-driven environment. This change enhances the ability to both innovate and disrupt, because earnings are not a focal point until much later in the life cycle of the company. The life cycle of a successful venture capital company has changed. Figure 3.6 shows the average age of a successful company to go public in 2000 was six years, and the average acquisition time frame four years. This life cycle has almost doubled, because venture capital firms maintain private ownership longer.

The term *unicorn* was coined to designate a venture-backed company with an equity valuation greater than $1 billion. Prior to the 2008 financial crisis, unicorns were practically nonexistent. Any company with a valuation approaching $1 billion would have entered the public markets to access capital and create liquidity. Now, ven-ture capital funds are so large they can sustain companies longer privately and absorb more losses. Managing a company for profit is something that can be pushed into the future. Figure 3.7 illustrates US venture capital invested in unicorns on an annual

FIGURE 3.6   Average time being held privately of venture capital backed companies

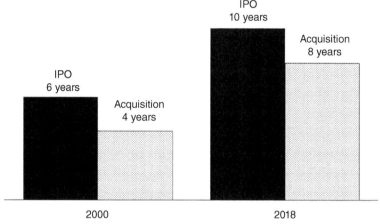

FIGURE 3.7   US venture capital invested in unicorns (billions $US)

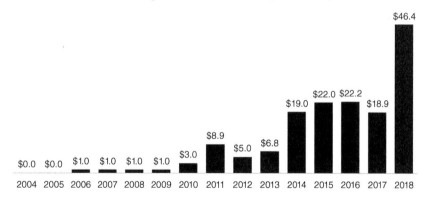

basis. In 2018, $46.4 billion was invested in companies with an equity valuation greater than $1 billion. Ten years ago that number was less than $5 billion.

Reviewing the initial public offering activity, in Figure 3.8, it is clear that companies are staying private longer. There is no longer the need to access capital publicly for the allure of being a public company. As Figure 3.8 illustrates, the 2010s saw the lowest number of new IPOs in many decades. In addition to having very few IPOs, the profitability of those IPOs was very low. The solid line in the chart below tracks the percentage of companies that are profitable on their IPO date. In 2019, 81% of the companies that came public were unprofitable. That level of negative earnings for

FIGURE 3.8   Initial public offerings (IPOs)

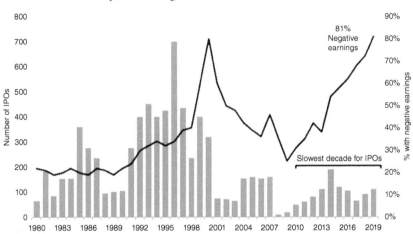

companies has not been seen since the dot-com era. These are all indications that the capital markets are allowing companies to focus on taking market share over profits.

A portion of the risk capital coming into new ventures is coming from public companies hoping to find the next industry disruptor themselves before, or at least alongside, venture capitalists. Through corporate subsidiaries, public companies have created their own venture arms to try and foster innovation both synergistically and totally independently of their core enterprise. Prior to the 2008 financial crisis, these corporate venture capital funds held between $5 billion and $10 billion. Today the number has reached $66 billion, as much as a ten times increase. Corporate venture funds were involved in 51% of all venture capital deals in 2018, a significant increase from 25% ten years ago. Figure 3.9 demonstrates the significant increase in corporate interest in venture capital.

FIGURE 3.9   US corporate venture capital raised (billions $US)

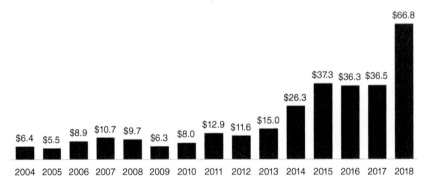

Venture success leads to financially successful entrepreneurs and investors, which leads to a greater supply of young, eager innovators willing to take chances and spend their time on new ideas. Human capital focuses on innovation increases, when financial capital is successful.

In June 2019, 26% of the companies in the broad Russell 3000 US Index had zero earnings. With the exception of the 2008 financial crisis period (when investors did want profits, but they were scarce), that is the highest percentage of unprofitable companies in the index ever. Additionally many companies are profitable, but they are trading at very high valuation multiples as they invest in growth internally. Amazon, the most prominent disruptor, threatens every industry vertically and has the capital and backing of Wall Street to take large losses during the disruption period.

All this capital focused on innovation has materially accelerated the pace of technology and with it disruption. This significant innovation cycle probably does not sound like a bad outcome for society, and from many perspectives it is quite positive. I hope society reaps long-term benefits despite some shorter-term challenges of necessary new regulations and the growing pains of change. Unfortunately, viewed through the lens of a fundamental public equity markets investors, it brings many challenges. Any time the financial markets move away from the analysis of cash flow and paradigm shifts become common, fundamental investors will struggle.

Outperformance potential with unprofitable but disruptive companies?

One might say, the innovation cycle is clear: just buy companies with new technologies that are growing fast and hold on for great future success. That may work for the very top venture capital firms, but it has never been a winning strategy in the public equity markets. Venture capital company selection is more art than science, more vision then due diligence. The venture capital portfolio strategy is to invest behind 10 to 20 ideas and hope one or two of them grow into the next Google, Facebook, or Uber. The other 18 companies will go bankrupt or struggle for years hoping to return some small amount of capital. This strategy is very profitable for the top quintile of venture capital firms that can attract the top entrepreneurs and use their extensive human capital relationships to add value. Many lower-tier venture capital firms struggle, because their big winners are never quite big enough to cover the bankruptcies and they have fewer companies bought out at premium valuations.

Venture capital is one of the very few financial investment classes where one investor's dollar is worth more than another investor's. When individuals open their personal brokerage account and buy public company stock, they get the same price as the biggest asset manager in the world. The market is generally liquid and egalitarian. Although some activist or constructionist public investment firms may try to add value to the public companies they invest in, generally the management team succeeds or fails on their own. For 90+% of public equity investors, their value contribution to their portfolio companies is zero.

Venture capital (VC) investments are accessible only to the parties invited by the management team to negotiate in the potential investment. An investment from one of the premier VC firms is worth more to an entrepreneur than an investment from a local VC firm. A premier VC firm financial backing adds prestige to the young company and opens doors that would not otherwise open for the entrepreneurs. The VC market is not liquid or egalitarian. VC investing methodologies and processes will not work in the public markets

For a short period of time when markets are hot and capital is plentiful, greed will be the emotion of the day on Wall Street and high growth, potentially disruptive stocks, will outperform. This was the case in the 2010s. Unfortunately, through cycles, a strategy of investing in these stocks in the public markets will not succeed for very quantitative reasons.

> *Too much capital availability makes money flow to the wrong places.*
> *—Howard Marks*

First, by the time a company goes public it is not a secret. If they have a new technology or some exciting innovation, it is very well publicized. The company and its investors will make sure it is well publicized, because they are trying to get the best valuation possible when going public. This communication and (again) the egalitarian process of buying public stock mean an exciting new company will receive a very high valuation. By definition of buying at a very high valuation, you will not be able to extract the huge gain that a VC investor receives from a portfolio winner, because they were invested before the company was proven affording them a significantly lower valuation. The big winner for the venture capitalist that creates returns for their entire portfolio is often a 100 times and higher return. You are not going to receive that type of return in the public markets. Although the public markets are not strongly efficient, they are clearly much more efficient than private illiquid markets. Second, sheer size becomes a factor. When you invest in a company with $5 million in revenues, you might see it grow revenues 200 times and reach $1 billion in seven years, but if you invest in a public company with $1 billion in revenues, there is very little chance of seeing revenues reach $200 billion in seven years.

For these reasons, a public portfolio of all the high-growth, and therefore high-valuation stocks, will not outperform through cycles. The key here is through cycles. Growth companies can create outperformance if invested in at the right times and right points in a cycle. If you have done research on a high-growth company and get the opportunity to buy during a time when investors have become fearful of the future (causing a lower relative valuation), this may be a compelling, outperforming strategy. Taking a contrarian view and buying an asset at a reasonable valuation of its projected growth trajectory is potentially a good idea. It is the indiscriminate buying at any valuation that will not work over time. The outperformance we are focused on in these discussions is a repeatable, consistent outperformance *through* business and market cycles. It is, of course, possible to outperform with almost any strategy, if you time the market correctly, but generally this is not a consistent repeatable strategy. After monitoring hundreds of hedge fund managers over the years, it is only a small minority (maybe 5%) that demonstrate the ability to market time correctly over a long career.

Private markets overheating?

When you combine the VC growth discussed previously with the massive increase in private equity firm capital, there is real concern that private market valuations are becoming frothy to the point of disappointing investors. The low public market rate environment has caused many investors who do not usually have large allocations to private equity to increase their allocations in a search for higher returns. In Figure 3.10 detailing private equity dollars awaiting deployment you can see that we are at historic highs. At over $600 billion, private equity looking for opportunities has tripled in five years.

In a number of institutional capital allocator surveys in 2019, private equity ranked number one as the asset class in which they expect to increase investment over the next few years. Illiquidity is a risk and that risk is being discounted today by a large number of investors trying to meet their investment mandates.

FIGURE 3.10   Private equity dry powder (billions $US)

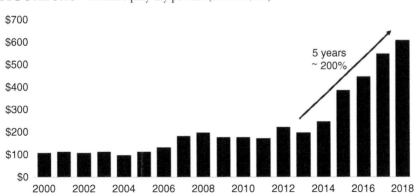

Contrarianism and paradigm shifts

Investing in a contrary fashion to the current shorter-term trends and beliefs of the market is important to creating sustainable long-term outperformance and goes hand in hand with the ability to invest with a longer time horizon than the average investor. Investors cannot put capital behind a contrarian thesis if their thesis is not given the time to play out or if there is a high probability of a paradigm shift. The necessary time horizon to be compensated for being a contrarian has been analyzed in a number of ways, but three to five years has historically been enough time to comfortably invest behind a contrarian thesis.

The following cycle has been the challenge in the 2010s. Momentum investors have prospered and any form of value or fundamental investing has struggled. There will come a point where this cycle will break and investors will begin to lose money and start to demand earnings again. As of June 2019, we have still not reached that point.

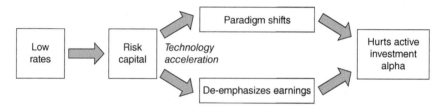

The result of this cycle for an entire decade has been a massive increase in capital allocation to passive investing. Allocators have lost faith in active managers' ability to create alpha and become momentum oriented themselves by moving capital into various passive investing alternatives. This trend to passive investing is global in nature.

CHAPTER 4

PASSIVE INVESTING

- *Factor investing*
- *How far can passive investing go?*
- *Are the losers quitting the game?*
- *Financial product creation and passive alternatives*

Capital allocators have been losing conviction in their belief that investment managers can create alpha and have become focused on fee reductions and passive investing alternatives. Almost $3 trillion went into passive alternatives in 2018, and a net $1.5 trillion left active funds. These massive fund outflows have continued in 2019 and create a negative cycle for active managers illustrated below.

As active managers see allocators moving capital to passive investing, they have little choice but to try and stem the flow by trying to demonstrate outperformance immediately. Short-term thinking and decision-making inevitably lead to poor performance. In the market environment of 2019, short-term decision-making translates into buying high-growth stocks, because they have momentum. Popular growth stocks are bought regardless of valuation and the core tenets of cash flow analysis and contrarianism are cast aside. Ultimately this will cause negative performance for those active managers unable to abstain from following the herd and chasing a momentum-driven market to try and keep their investor base.

We have not yet seen how the markets will react in a major drawdown, when a very large percentage of assets are in passive vehicles. Illustrated in Figure 4.1, 51% of all assets under management are now in passive investments. This is an increase from 20% of assets in 2009 to about 50% in 2020, a 250% increase in ten years. At the core of this trend is the decade-long reign of central bank intervention. As individual company investment decisions are surpassed by macro-driven models

FIGURE 4.1   Percentage of overall equity investments in passive vehicles 2009 to October 2019

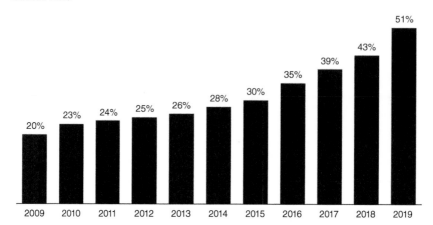

and asset class–level portfolio-allocation decisions, the markets will increasingly become momentum driven.

When (not if) the economy enters a recession or some other catalyst sparks a major market drawdown, how will capital allocators react in regards to their passive investments?

For many capital allocators, there will no longer be as many investment manager relationships to call for support and guidance. Capital allocators will not have fundamental analysis to fall back on, because passive investing is much more akin to macro investing than fundamental investing. You do not own a company, you own "all companies." It is much easier for most people to envision the value and worth of a single company and its asset value, brands, and other intangible barriers to entry than to envision the value of the S&P 500. Similarly, it is easier for allocators to have conviction in trusted manager relationships that have been built over years than to have conviction to stay the course in an equity index. The buying and selling of passive investments are inherently momentum oriented and the market will be much more susceptible to investor herding.

Will allocators hold onto their passive investments when the markets start to drop or will they become unconscious trend followers and sell assets creating herding and a further downward spiral?

It will be completely rational, expected human behavior to decide to sell your S&P 500 index ETF position, when everyone else is selling their positions. If you were going to sell an S&P 500 ETF based on valuation alone, you would have sold in 2015, yet the market went up another 50%. At any time in history, market pundits can use macro data to predict the market will go up or down in convincing fashion. The Federal Reserve is lowering rates, because the economy is slowing. Do you sell because the economy is slowing or buy because rates are being lowered? The answer is going to be very dependent on how the markets react to the news, and that is the definition of herding and the best way to achieve poor performance.

> *You hear these people on television saying the market has told them this and that—well, the market has never spoken to me.*
>
> —*Julian Robertson, investor*

We also have not seen how liquidity will be affected in times of a stressful drawdown, when passive entities own major portions of the float (tradeable shares outstanding) of almost all US stocks. The Vanguard Group with over $5 trillion in assets under management is the largest provider of mutual funds and the second largest provider of exchange traded funds (Blackrock is the number one provider of exchange traded funds). Shown in Figure 4.2, Vanguard through its passive vehicles controls over 5% or more of the float of 99.8% of US publicly traded equities. This is an increase from only 21% of US equities in 2010, a 500% increase in a decade. When allocators invest passively, they buy everything regardless of value, and when they sell, everything will be sold, regardless of value. Vanguard does not understand (or care about) the value of the companies of which it owns 5+% of the tradeable shares. Vanguard buys or sells the entire market when money flows in and out of their passive investment offerings. Individual industry or company characteristics do not come into the equation.

FIGURE 4.2   Percentage of US equities in which Vanguard owns more than 5% of the outstanding float 2010 to October 2019

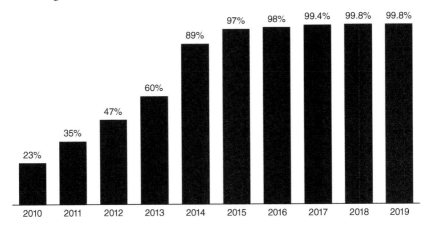

Indiscriminate selling or buying should create opportunities for active investors who are able to manage their process and invest with the key investment tenets. However time horizons will again be challenged, because herding takes time to work itself through the market. The most recent example of extreme herding in US markets was the dot-com bubble in 2000. If you recognized the extreme buying and investor herding mentality in internet stocks in 1998, it took three years before you were proven right during the crash. Many fundamental investors produced their worst returns during the dot-com era, because their fundamental analysis kept them away from buying stocks during the craze. If they were **short** internet stocks, the exponential rise was too strong to manage and fundamental managers often had to cover shorts before they were proven right.

When the investment industry talks about *bubbles,* the insinuation is that there is irrational buying occurring that will stop and reverse in dramatic fashion (*pop*) at some point. Passive investing itself is not a classic bubble, because its existence and increased use is not irrational by certain market constituents, and it does not have to end in dramatic fashion. However, it is a trend and financial investment vehicle that will have major implications for equity markets in the future. The momentum nature of passive investing will cause fundamental cash flow and contrarian investment decision-making to take longer (extend time horizons) to be proven right. So although passive investing will not all of a sudden stop and go out of favor, its effect will be felt on markets and fundamental active investors.

> *There are two requirements for success in Wall Street. One you have to think correctly; and secondly you have to think independently.*
>
> —Ben Graham

Factor investing

Factor strategies, a form of passive investing, are diversified equity portfolios that represent a specific **systematic risk** and return characteristic. The portfolio is created by screening a large universe of equities for specific financial or price data that is believed to represent the risk and return characteristics desired. For instance, one of the earliest factor strategies was designed to highlight the "value factor." Price-to-book ratio of each company in the universe was used to determine which companies were low value and which were high value. The universe would be sorted by price-to-book ratio and the top quintile (cheapest) and bottom quintile (most expensive) were analyzed over time to determine if alpha was created by holding cheap stocks. Much academic research has shown the value factor to demonstrate low levels of alpha creation over the history of the US financial markets. However, there have been very long periods when it demonstrates negative alpha creation, and this current environment is one of those periods. Many of the challenges from low rates and tech disruption directly apply to the value factors' ability to create alpha.

Theoretically, you can create hundreds of factor strategies based on the financial and price metrics of a universe of companies. Academic research has been done on more than 75 different factor strategies. In reality many of them will be so correlated to each other that they will not be of any value. The original factors found to offer unique risk and return characteristics are value, momentum, and quality. Additional metrics that have demonstrated alpha potential to screen on and create portfolios are free cash flow, low **beta,** high yield, dividend growth, and market cap size.

Although a number of different factor strategies have been studied in academia for decades, they have only been widely adopted by large capital allocators in the 2010s. The primary reason for factor strategy adoption during this time is capital allocators' quest to add some value to their benchmark return. As allocators have lost faith in individual active investment managers and moved capital to passive investments, they search for some alpha above an ETF index, which exactly represented their benchmark. Factor strategies offer a low-fee way to potentially create a small amount of alpha with low tracking error.

It is unclear whether factor investing will add value for the average capital allocator over time, but it is clear that factor alternatives have become distorted, and many allocators do not really know what they own. As we have discussed, low rates pushed allocators into larger holdings of equity exposure than would be normal. In response, low beta factor strategies were created to offer allocators a lower risk equity return stream. Beta is the measure of systematic risk in a stock in comparison to the entire market. Stocks with betas lower than 1.0 have a lower volatility than the market. These stocks would be expected to be safer, when risk is defined by volatility. This became a misleading strategy in the 2010s and demonstrates why solely defining risk as volatility is not a comprehensive risk measurement analysis. When low rates created demand for high-growth stocks, they began to outperform the market. Because it was so widely accepted that high-growth stocks were the best place to invest, the stocks demonstrated a lower volatility than the market. When beta was measured (volatility in relation to the market), high-growth stocks were screened to be low beta. Low beta factor strategies held companies that were clearly not "safer"; they were simply stocks displaying lower beta over the period that was being measured. The market environment of the 2010s distorted many factor strategies, which will commonly happen over short time periods.

Factor strategies can be additive to an allocator's returns, if understood and used for the right purposes. They are not a panacea for the low alpha creation problem, and any time very large amounts of capital enter strategies there will be market distortions.

How far can passive investing go?

Japan is the great experiment in terms of central bank intervention and fund flows into passive investing. As of December 2019, the Japanese stock market had 71% of all equity assets under management invested in passive funds (20% higher than the United States). Passive funds rule the Japanese equity market. Unfortunately we cannot learn many passive investing lessons from the Japanese stock market, because the Bank of Japan (BOJ) has distorted their markets beyond the point of the Fed or ECB. The Bank of Japan does not just buy Japanese Government Bonds (JGBs), as other central banks do, to manipulate interest rates. The BOJ has been buying equities through passive Japanese equity ETFs since the 2008 financial crisis to try and support financial markets. In 2018, the BOJ bought $55 billion of Japanese passive equity ETFs and now holds 80% of all the outstanding assets in passive ETFs. The BOJ owns over 50% of all Japanese sovereign debt (JGBs) and 50% of the float in Japan's equity markets. Japan's chief bank governor, Abe Kuroda, has been questioned on this equity market manipulation, but he still claims the BOJ's buying is not distorting valuations. Abe's defense would be that Japanese equity valuations are at globally low levels, so the BoJ's buying program could not be artificially increasing valuations. If BoJ equity purchases are not supporting the Japanese equity markets then why not let them trade to their market-driven level? Figure 4.3 illustrates the history of passive investments in Japan.

Only time will tell where this will end for Japan, but it most likely will have little to do with fundamental analysis and the other investment tenets that lead to active management outperformance. Global macro issues affecting the Japanese currency and internal bank of Japan fiscal and monetary policies will be the key drivers, more so than fundamental company analysis.

This trend to passive investing should be worrisome, because it is a movement away from the inherent reason the equity markets exist and investors invest. Equity markets exist to provide capital to companies who need that capital to grow and have demonstrated an economic value or future potential to investors. Investors should be

FIGURE 4.3   Percentage of passive investments in Japanese equity accounts (BoJ holdings included) 2004 to October 2019

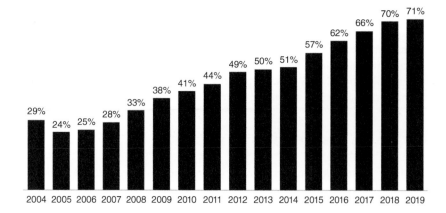

investing to provide capital to these deserving companies, so that they may achieve a return on their capital and be a participant in the future of the company in which they invested. Passive investing may still provide capital during strong macro-economic times, because investors will buy ETFs, but it will be an indiscriminate source of capital. Over longer periods of time, an indiscriminate source of capital is not efficient or productive. We have moved away from the original economic purpose of the equity market, when ETFs rule the market.

Are the losers quitting the game?

Many experts see investment decision-making and active investing as a zero sum game. Each trade or active decision creates a winner and loser in the marketplace. There is strong evidence to suggest that the consistent losers are unsophisticated retail, individual, small investors. In Figure 4.4, JP Morgan Asset Management calculates returns since 1998 by major asset classes and then calculates the return of the average American small investor. As you can see, the average investor return is 1.9% annually, which is below every other asset class.

If JP Morgan's average investor calculation is correct, it demonstrates that the average small investor is destroying value on a consistent basis. The average investor, before passive alternatives arose, invested their money by either picking individual stocks themselves through brokers or by picking mutual fund managers. Both these methods of investment created below-market returns.

There are two major ways to achieve a return below every other asset class. The first is by paying high fees. We know that individual investors have historically paid

FIGURE 4.4   20-year annualized returns by asset class 1998 to 2018

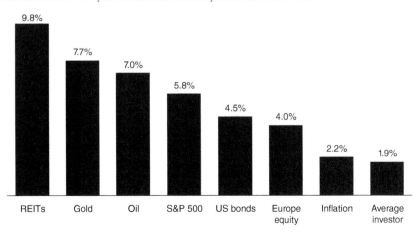

high fees without commensurate returns, so fees are certainly part of the equation. However, if we were to add back 200 basis points annually (a hefty fee premium) to the return it would increase it to 3.9%, a return still below the lowest performing asset class.

The second way to destroy value is through bad active investment decisions. These would come in the form of either poorly timing asset allocation changes or poor security selection. This type of value destruction would help other more sophisticated investors outperform. There are many data points that suggest individual investors *buy high and sell low*. It is very common for individual investors to pick the best-performing asset class or mutual fund manager on a three-year return basis and to change course when they have a bad year or two in the markets. This is a strategy that guarantees a poor outcome. Individual investors, also, continually fall victim to the behavioral pitfalls, which we will discuss in future chapters.

Clearly, individual retail investors have provided sophisticated active managers with the opportunity to outperform the market. Unfortunately, it is very difficult to account for the exact source and magnitude of individual investor loss. The question of whether this massive move to passive investing by small investors is making outperformance harder for sophisticated investors because the losers have left the marketplace is difficult to analyze. It is a question worth following, but will take a long time to truly determine.

Figure 4.4 clearly illustrates why individual non-sophisticated investors should invest passively. It is an intelligent choice. This small, individual investor underperformance does raise another question.

Why do individual investors not reallocate their personal individual stock holdings and mutual fund holdings to sophisticated active managers, as opposed to the passive investing trend?

The reason is that individual investors do not have the time, knowledge, or access to pick good investment managers. Picking above-average investment managers is a unique skill set in itself. More directly, the very best managers in the world are prohibited from advertising to, and accepting monies from, non-high net worth investors. Due to the lack of regulation and potential volatility, the government has put access to private investment management firms beyond the reach of the small investor. This leads to there not being a good active management alternative for small investors even if they had the time and knowledge to pick the best managers.

The additional reason is that many small investors thought they were allocating to good active managers when they chose mutual funds and high-fee brokerage firms. The small investor investment experience is a primary driver in the move to passive investing. The mutual fund industry evolved into an asset-gathering, fee-generating industry that added no incremental value over time. The industry's inability to create outperformance was due to a focus on asset gathering, which led to a focus on tracking error (volatility of the index return) over outperformance. Additionally, many regulations handcuffed mutual fund management teams making outperformance more difficult and the cost of running a mutual fund to be high. These two issues combined caused a massive human capital move from the mutual fund industry to the private investment fund industry in prior decades.

Financial product creation and passive alternatives

Wall Street is a great innovator and has created many financially engineered products to achieve a specific return stream with risk and reward characteristics that will aid investors in achieving their mandate. Financially engineered products are the simple process of providing a customer a product. The new innovation is always based on an extraction, manipulation, or combination of original products that have a market-driven use. Tranche-ing and repackaging debt and credit default swaps are separating out the return and risk characteristics of a larger portfolio of assets (that are actually providing some service in the economy) to create a specific return stream for an investor. This all makes perfect sense until the financially engineered product begins to overwhelm the market it is based on. Basically when the tail begins to wag the dog there is going to be a problem. In hindsight, it is very clear how these financially engineered products became a crisis in 2008: the financial engineering took on a life of its own outstripping the original assets that provided an economic use (mortgage origination). The economic value of mortgage creation became secondary to creating a product to sell to investors. Passive alternatives may be far from this point, but they are a manipulation of the original reason to make an equity investment.

The equity markets exist to fund individual companies based on their potential return and need for capital. Passive alternatives were created to allow small investors the ability to easily invest in all companies, because they could not spend the time or take the risk of choosing companies individually and, as we discussed previously, they were achieving significantly substandard returns. High-fee and substandard mutual fund performance demanded the market create some better alternative for retail investors.

Creating an exchange-traded product that would allow individual investors to buy a package of equities rather than buy one share of every company was providing a service based on efficiency and collecting a fee. The service was originally marketed to a small group of equity investors: individual retail accounts. For these individual retail investors, it is a value-added financial innovation. However today, ETFs are being embraced by very large, sophisticated investment allocators with billions of dollars in capital.

When that efficiency-driven service innovation accepts large amounts of capital and begins to drive the markets there can be a potential problem. Large institutional investors now use passive alternatives to achieve some projected theoretical market return that has a risk and reward characteristic that seems advantageous to a mean variance portfolio model. It is no longer a small slice of the equity volume. The size of the passive ETF market has the potential to become a tool that can be quickly bought and sold affecting all companies indiscriminately by driving equity **correlations** to 1.0 in times of stress.

It is unclear the effect passive investing will have on the markets in the future. Today, the effect is felt by active managers being forced to make short-term decisions to maintain their asset bases. It is, also, one of the causal agents in lengthening the time needed for individual company, fundamental investment decisions to be proven correct further pressuring active management.

In the future it may come to have a greater effect on the overall volatility of the market. Passive investing is momentum investing and momentum investing at its *extreme* is herding and herding creates bubbles and crashes. It has been demonstrated over and over in financial market history that humans overreact both positively and negatively. Having a majority of the market be invested in a momentum-based tool will amplify human decisions.

> *We've had a movement away from value investing to momentum investing, where price is not a factor. I can't tell you how many good investors really believe that price no longer matters, and that's not my style.*
>
> —*Julian Robertson, investor*

CHAPTER 5

THE 2020s

- *Economic drivers of the 2020s*
- *Continuation of technology-driven disruption*
- *American dream*
- *Populism*
- *Biggest downside risk: Loss of faith in central banks*
- *Consequences for active investing*
- *Is value investing dead?*

Given the effect of low rates and the pace of technology on active investors and the market, as a whole, it is important to step back and think about what the 2020s will bring. Forecasting macro events is difficult, and fundamental investors would prefer to focus on their businesses. However, it's necessary to think about what the markets will be facing and how major trends will affect businesses. Long-term investors can invest through decade-long trends with the hope of finding companies with tailwinds, not headwinds.

In 2009, the US was facing a major crisis in the banking system, weak financial markets, high unemployment, consumer stress driven by housing, and high deficits and debt levels. Historic measures were necessary. Low rates and quantitative easing were the only way to try and avoid a true economic depression. Dropping rates to zero and buying mortgages were unprecedented Federal Reserve measures, but people were desperate, scared, and willing to accept any economic answer. Globally since 2009, central banks have bought over $15 trillion of assets and made 713 rate cuts. These financial measures helped pull the global economy out of a dire situation. In 2019, financial institutions, the housing market, and the consumer are all stronger. Financial assets had the decade they needed to stabilize the economy annualizing over 13% annually and volatility was low.

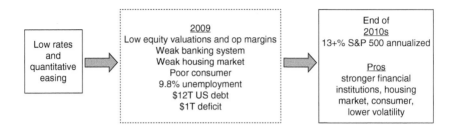

Economic drivers of the 2020s

The economic and business drivers in the 2020s will once again be led by low rates and accelerated technology disruption. These trends are too strong to stop and will continue through the next decade, but the outcome will be different due to the starting point. The positive is that the US economy is on a stronger foundation with a de-levered and fully functioning financial system. Unfortunately rates will not be able to be increased to historic norms due to a lack of economic growth.

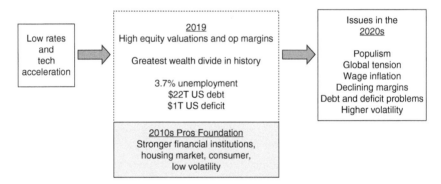

If there is a slowdown in the next decade, the Federal Reserve will not be able to effect the same rate of change, because rates are already historically low. The other potential instrument of growth—fiscal policy—has been a weak factor, as political polarization is at historic highs. In the 2020s, even if political parties align to try and use fiscal policies, the size of the current deficit and overall debt load will be a major factor in limiting their ability. US debt levels have grown to $22 trillion from $12 trillion in 2009, an 80% increase. Although gross domestic product (GDP) has grown during that period, the percentage of federal debt to GDP is at historic highs. In Figure 5.1, you can see that debt as a percentage of GDP has increased from about 60% in 2008 to over 100% today. Debt levels and budget deficits have been issues that garnered very little attention in the 2010s.

Debt levels and deflation will be significant fears in a recession, as debtors lose in a deflationary environment. Paying back loans with dollars that are harder to earn

FIGURE 5.1   Percentage of US federal debt to GDP 2000 to Q2 2019

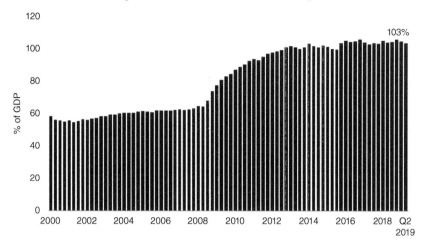

(due to deflation) would be a major problem for both the American consumer and the US government.

There are only two ways to pay down debt comfortably: growth in incomes or inflation. Inflation has been a major casualty of the acceleration of technology and paradigm shifts that make goods and services cheaper. Pushing the economy to increase demand beyond supply is difficult because technology advances cause efficiencies that aid production and drop prices. Despite decent US economic growth and the lowering of interest rates in the 1990s and 2000s, globalization kept inflation in check allowing for cheaper goods and a strong supply of commodities. As the productivity and cost cutting gains from globalization began to abate in the 2010s, inflation was kept in check by the accelerated pace of technology. The ability for technology advances to provide cheaper goods and services will continue to be a weight on inflation increases in the 2020s.

Economic growth will be difficult to create in the US, because it has been pulled forward for the last 20 years and now faces both exhaustion and aging demographics. Economic growth was pulled forward in the 2000s when houses were built well beyond capacity and consumers bought goods beyond their income capacity due to easy credit. When the markets collapsed in 2008, the only way to save the economy was to pull growth forward once again. Even lower rates and even easier credit spurred consumers to spend beyond their means once again. As occurred in the 2000s, credit was once again the driver of consumption in the 2010s. The housing market was stabilized by the government buying mortgages, lowering mortgage rates by over 250 basis points, and supporting lenders to lend for both new mortgages and home equity lines. Pulling demand forward is a short-term fix for real sustainable consumer spending growth.

Most consumer discretionary purchases have a wide range of time when the purchase is actually necessary. Consumers may need to replace their automobile every seven years, but they will purchase one every five years in a good employment environment and if cheap financing is available. However, if the environment changes and they feel unsure of the future and their financial prospects, they can wait for ten years to make the same purchase. The same thought process exists for everything from home furniture to electronics. When demand is pulled forward, the potential for a long period of sustained consumer austerity grows. During the 2010s consumers spent liberally spurred by a strong employment backdrop and cheap financing. If either one of those elements were to change, it would be very easy for consumers to slow spending without hardship, as they have recently replaced their discretionary purchases.

On the positive side, the American consumer's balance sheet has been strengthened since the trough of the 2008 financial crisis, but it has all been driven through inflated asset prices. Demand and consumption have materially outpaced income gains for two decades. Economic growth and inflation will benefit from the continued Federal Reserve support and potentially fiscal policy, but the headwinds of technology, demographics, and two decades of overconsumption by the US consumer will be difficult to overcome.

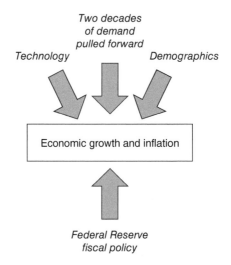

Continuation of technology-driven disruption

The accelerated pace of technology will continue to create disruption and paradigm shifts within industries in the 2020s. The number of companies disappearing will increase due to the combination of disruption and a slower economy that will take place. Companies in fact have already been dying at ever-quickening rates. There are two factors that affect a company's life span: disruption and health of the economy.

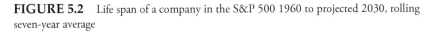

FIGURE 5.2   Life span of a company in the S&P 500 1960 to projected 2030, rolling seven-year average

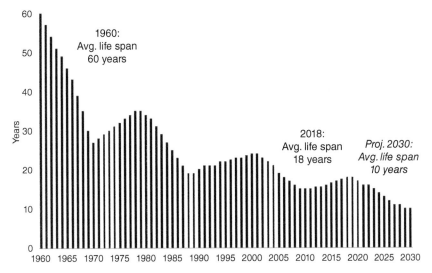

As shown in Figure 5.2, since 1960 52% of the S&P 500 companies have disappeared and the average life span is dropping. Back in 1960, the average life span of a company in the S&P 500 was 60 years. In 2018, due to increased disruption, the average life span dropped to 18 years. The 18-year life span is artificially high today, because the credit environment has been so strong. Some companies have remained solvent that will not survive the next recession. Finding sustainable business models will continue to be a pressure on individual security selection.

Technology driving business efficiency is not new, but the 2020s will see an elevated level of technology-created business efficiencies. These gains will be seen in the operating cost structure of companies across industries and in sales and marketing productivity. The driver will be the use of data. The 2010s was the infancy and growth of data collection and the 2020s will begin to truly harness and use that data for business productivity.

A Bank of America Global Research report on the growth in data collection reported that a US city with one million citizens will produce (and have collected) 200 million gigabytes of data per day. Data collection metrics are difficult to understand for non-technocrats, so to give some context, the average Apple iPhone holds between 16 and 64 gigabytes. If we assume we have the average 32 GB iPhone, the data collected in a US city with one million people will account for 6,250,000 iPhones per day. Across the entire US that equates to about 2,000,000,000 iPhones full of data daily. The increase in data capture has been exponential over the last ten years with experts estimating that 90% of all the world's data was collected in the last two years. Data storage cost per gigabyte has dropped from $9.00 in 2000 to $0.01 in 2018; this is exponential technology-driven deflation. Despite the exponential increase in data collection in the 2010s, business productivity did not exponentially increase, because how, when, and where to use the data is just being developed. In the 2020s, business productivity will be significantly affected by the use of the data being collected, causing lower cost structures and better sales productivity.

> *The pace of change and the threat of disruption creates tremendous opportunities.*
> *—Steve Case, technology CEO*

The second major effect of accelerated technology in the 2020s will be the increase in automation. Automation was also in its infancy in the 2010s and advances in robotics combined with the increased data collection will advance the use of automation across almost all industries. Automation will be a boost for business earnings, but amplify social problems. Automation and the continued pace of technology generally will continue to put pressure on the negative social externality of the widening wealth and education gap in America.

Technology advances lowering operating costs will produce downward pressure on inflation. As globalization levels off and there are potential decreases due to global trade tensions, technology advances will be the largest pressure on inflation allowing rates to remain low. The only potential for significantly increased inflation will be exogenous geopolitical shocks, such as wars, commodity embargos, or major cross-border capital constraints.

American dream

The decisions made by the Federal Reserve in pursuit of stabilizing the economy in the 2010s may have been unavoidable. Unfortunately the derivative effects of low rates inflating asset prices and of technology advances pressuring old economy workers has had negative social effects. The major social problem is the creation of the greatest wealth divide in the United States since the 1920s. This wealth divide is compounded by an education divide affecting the same demographic group.

Americans that did not own financial assets were left behind financially in the 2010s. This same group of nonfinancial-asset-owning Americans have been competitively left behind due to a lack of education, primarily in science and technology. It's a vicious cycle to try and break out of for the bottom half of Americans. In Figure 5.3, you can see that the probability of going to college is about 250% higher for the top quintile of parent wealth households compared to the bottom quintile. Financial wealth drives education. Education drives financial wealth. Asset owners prosper and workers subsist.

The roots of the American culture are in realizing the American dream, but the realization of moving up the socioeconomic ladder has been declining, and the 2010s

FIGURE 5.3   Probability of going to college by parent income rank

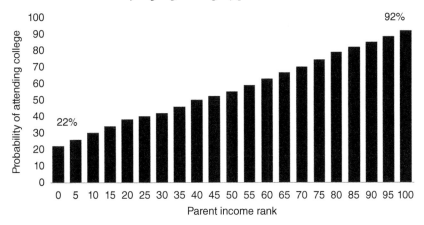

FIGURE 5.4   Probability that children are better off than parents

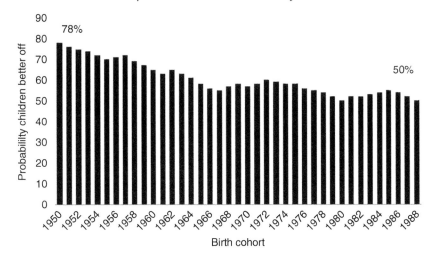

accelerated that decline. In Figure 5.4 an analysis by the Brookings Institute highlights the decline. Today, there is only a 50% chance that children will be better off than their parents. In 1950, there was a 78% chance children would be better off than their parents. This decline is exasperated when analyzed by region of the country. Americans in the Deep South and Midwest are much less likely to achieve higher socioeconomic status. The US does not even compare well to other countries. In a 2018 Brookings Institute report by Richard Reeves titled "Few American are making more than their parents did ... ," the probability of a US citizen moving from the bottom quintile in household income (about $24,500 in the US) to the top quintile (about $220,000 in the US) was 7.5% compared to 9.0% in the UK and 13.5% in Canada.

This wealth and education divide will be further pressured in the 2020s as the government must continue to support asset prices to avoid a downward recessionary cycle and maintain inflation. Technological automation, robotics, and data use will have a positive effect on productivity but a negative effect on employment and the wages of manufacturing and service workers. These factors will continue to economically pressure the same group that was left behind in the 2010s.

Populism

The effect of the widening wealth divide, educational divide, and the disruption of traditional industries by technology and globalization will create a strong trend toward populism and nationalism. Populism has begun to grow globally in the last few years and will continue to pick up as pressure on the middle class working demographic continues in the 2020s.

The median US household has an income of $62,000, a net worth of $95,000, and some college or an associates' degree. This is not the economic demographic group that has been uplifted during the 2010s. They were supported in the sense that the Federal Reserve actions stopped the recession in 2008 from going deeper and causing more job losses and credit defaults. However, the people in this group are only very marginally stronger financially than they were a decade ago. Stopping things from getting worse, as the Federal Reserve did during the 2008 financial crisis and continues to do through market intervention, is not readily apparent to middle class workers. What is more visible is the top quintile of American income producers growing their net worth almost 200% during the decade after the financial crisis. The net worth of the top 1% of Americans has surpassed the entire net worth of all middle class Americans (defined as the second, third, and fourth quintiles ranked by net worth).

Driven by both monetary policy and tax reform, the top quintile of Americans and corporate America were the significant winners in the 2010s. Corporations were aided by low rates, easy credit conditions, tax reform, and lower regulation. The Department of Justice (DoJ) investigations into monopolies, mergers, and anti-competition are at a historic low. In the 2010s, DoJ investigations dropped over 33%, and more industry oligopolies were created in the US than ever before in history. In 1995, the top 100 public companies accounted for 53% of all the income from publicly listed companies. In 2018, the top 100 public companies accounted for 85% of all publicly traded profits. Concentration of market share has occurred in almost every industry. Central bank intervention and fiscal policies after the 2008 financial crisis have actually accelerated the number of companies that are *too big to fail.*

Although the larger problem of breaking the cycle of education and wealth is beyond the scope here, the ramifications for the financial markets in the next decade are clear. The pendulum of power and profits has shifted to support of the top quintile of American earners and corporations to a historically high degree. This pendulum of power between asset owners and workers swings in decade-plus-long regimes, but it can only swing so far without counterforces affecting the balance. Increased regulation, taxes, social programs, unions, social unrest, and trade barriers are the balancing effects that will begin to gain support in the 2020s.

Populism gains momentum when middle class workers feel disenfranchised and unappreciated. The disenfranchised working class want more from the people they feel are above them socioeconomically and from those who may be equivalent socioeconomically, but are not seen as deserving. The undeserving group almost always involves foreigners who are perceived to be taking income and opportunity in some fashion. Populism turns into nationalism when disenfranchisement turns into an *us versus them* mentality. In the US today, this disenfranchisement can be seen in rising global tensions, immigration policies, and calls for increasing social programs financed by taxes on the wealthy.

Populism and nationalism are closely linked and both negatively affect the globalization trend that has been in effect since the 1990s. American businesses embraced global expansion and global supply chains in the 1990s, and a large share of US manufacturing was sent overseas to lower-wage countries between 1990 and 2010. The outcome was an increase in corporate profit margins and, importantly, very cheap goods for the American consumer. Today those supply chains are still healthy and intact, but the growth has slowed as most products that made sense to source overseas already have been outsourced.

The extent of increased regulations and taxes on American businesses and financial markets is as yet unknown. For active investors, the focus will be on valuation multiples and company profit margins. Net profit margins and cash creation will be the largest factor of change going forward, if globalization stalls and taxes increase.

Which external pressures will have the greatest effect on company profit margins?

From a profit margin perspective low rates will have little new effect, because those gains were reaped in the 2010s. The major positive force is technology and the efficiencies that have been discussed. Opposing the positive force of technology gains will be the end of globalization gains, increased regulation, increased social spending, and potentially concerns over deficit and debt levels leading to increased taxes. From 1980 to 2010, globalization was the most important factor in lowering the cost structures for American companies. As shown in Figure 5.5, global trade increased well over 50% for three decades. Growth was high in the 1980s and 1990s as companies began sourcing finished goods from low-cost countries. The greatest growth, almost 150%, occurred from 2000 to 2010 as advances in computer technology enabled American and European companies to build out their entire supply chains globally.

FIGURE 5.5   IMF world exports: Value of goods in billions of US$ 1970 to 2018

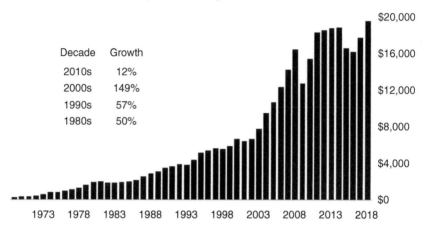

Decade	Growth
2010s	12%
2000s	149%
1990s	57%
1980s	50%

Supply chain technology advanced to the point that manufacturing companies could keep track of hundreds of individual parts being sourced from different countries. This enabled companies to find the cheapest source for each individual part. Inventory levels were lowered by almost all developed world companies, because technology enabled the advent of *just in time* manufacturing. New software technologies, better and faster emerging world shipping infrastructure, and low emerging world labor costs enabled great cost savings for companies in the developed world. This trend reached its peak and has slowed materially since 2010. The cost savings from globalization will not go away, but from a relative year over year comparable perspective there will not be new cost savings for American and European companies.

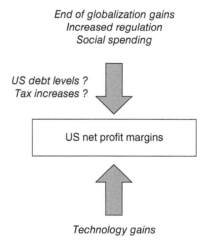

End of globalization gains
Increased regulation
Social spending

US debt levels ?
Tax increases ?

US net profit margins

Technology gains

As often happens, society reflects the externalities of business and economic changes years after they have actually occurred. This globalization trend caused manufacturing jobs to steadily disappear in the US for decades, but the tipping point that drives action takes a long time. The momentum of the blue collar American workers political agenda to lower global trade through tariffs and regulation gained traction in 2015. The previous graphic demonstrates that US profit margins will have downward pressure in the 2020s due to peaking of the globalization trend, but also due to increased regulation, tariffs, and social costs that have been driven by globalization-driven job loss in the past 30 years.

Another factor that may arise to pressure profit margins is the US debt load. In the last few years, the US and global investors have ignored the continually growing debt and deficit spending that exists even in a prospering US economy. The major reason for the lack of concern about US deficit and debt levels is the relative comparison to Europe and Japan. Were global investors to stop investing in countries with burgeoning debt levels, they would have no place to invest. The US is the best of a bad bunch in the developed world economies. Historically high deficits and debt levels are not a good place for populist-driven economic measures to start, because they almost always create even higher deficits and debt levels. Active investors will have to navigate the technology tailwinds and the headwinds of social issues affecting profit margins in the next decade

The biggest downside risk: Loss of faith in central banks

In reviewing the realm of possibilities coming in the 2020s, positioning a portfolio for a worst-case scenario is not good investment practice, but performing analysis to understand the worst-case scenario and the potential signs that may precede negative events is good practice. The worst scenario for the US in the next decade would be an economic recession combined with a loss of faith in central banks. The 2008 recession caused a crisis of faith in the global banking system. That crisis of faith was averted by financial support from global governments through central bank intervention. If not for central banks in 2008, we would have surely fallen into a global depression. If there is a crisis of faith in global central banks, there is no institution that can avert that crisis.

Economies would slow, tax revenues would drop, and government debt burdens would become the defining issue for investors. Sovereign debt markets could freeze up, as investors lose faith and decide lending governmental institutions money at 0% interest rates is not a good economic decision. Governmental services would have trouble continuing and tax rates would have to rise at the worst time, causing a downward cycle. This complete loss of faith in central banks and sovereign debt repayment is an unlikely scenario, but there are more likely tangential downside scenarios.

After a decade of anemic growth across the globe, despite 0% interest rates across most of the developed world, company executives may no longer feel confident in economic returns on capital and significantly pullback on capital expenditures. Sovereign debt markets may still function, but future guidance of 0% interest rates by central banks may not stir animal spirits in investors and company executives. Investors and corporations could both begin to hold more cash and become very risk averse despite easy credit. This scenario would still cause a deep global recession.

Historically, the Federal Reserve has lowered interest rates by 4.0% (400 basis points) during a recessionary period to spur economic growth. The 2020s begins in unchartered territory for global central banks and economies, because interest rates are too low to allow for a historically normal central bank lowering of rates. A number of Fed governors have discussed their expected ability to "talk" the markets back into stability without having to make actual rate cuts. They have come to believe that the recent history of investors hanging on every word and parsing every phrase of their releases will always continue in the future. Today they can move markets upward with a phrase about "remaining vigilant and supportive," as investors buy on any sign of Fed dovishness, but there is no guarantee that this will be the case in the future.

> *[In June 2014] I worry about the effectiveness of monetary policy in the next downturn.*
>
> —Ray Dalio, investor

In the 2010s, investors rejoiced in *the fed put,* which is the expectation that any time the equity markets falter or credit spreads widen, the Federal Reserve will come into the markets and offer support through lower rates or quantitative easing. The belief in central bank support is held not just in the US but also globally. There is always a buyer waiting on the other side of a trade, because the government cannot allow the start of a downward spiral and supporting the financial markets has become an unspoken additional mandate (inflation and unemployment are the two stated mandates). Europe's financial leader, Mario Draghi pulled the euro currency and the European economy out of crisis in 2011 by telling the markets that the European Central Bank (ECB) would do "whatever it takes" to support the economy and currency. Investors believed in the ECB's ability and the markets came roaring back. There has been more hope than substance in a European recovery. There could come a time when investors begin to believe the ECB does not have "what it takes" to spur economic growth.

As was previously stated, continually positioning for a worst-case scenario is a poor investment philosophy. There are too many unknown variables to account for in the future, but it is good to think through all scenarios, especially when investing in a late economic cycle environment with historically low interest rates.

> *You can't predict. You can prepare.*
>
> —Howard Marks, investor

Consequences for active investing

The implications of these trends for active managers in the 2020s are mixed. The continuation of technology-driven paradigm shifts and central bank interventions will pressure active management and most likely cause continued growth in passive investing alternatives. On the positive side, volatility and equity dispersion should increase as profit margins are affected and downward earnings revisions are more common than in the 2010s.

Central bank intervention in the 2010s drove historically low volatility despite the many global risks. Whether significant downside scenarios occur or not, there will be more recessionary scares and volatility will increase. The complacency of the 2010s will not be repeated, because the market awakens to the end of an economic cycle, high equity valuations, peak corporate margins, and central banks that will have less firepower than they had in the 2010s. The 2010s' average volatility level of 16.8 is the lowest in recent history. Additionally volatility spikes above 20 were rare. As seen in Figure 5.6, from 2010 to 2019 volatility was below the 20 level 79% of weeks compared to 50% in the 2000s and 67% in the 1990s.

Increased volatility will reward managers who remain disciplined, do not chase short-term performance, and invest in companies with strong cash flows. Strong cash flow and strong balance sheets were not rewarded in the 2010s, because volatility was low and financing cheap and easily accessible. Ranking stock return performance by highest to lowest free cash flow yield has historically demonstrated a predictive relationship, where higher free cash flow producing companies have better

FIGURE 5.6   US Volatility Index (VIX) 1990 to October 2019

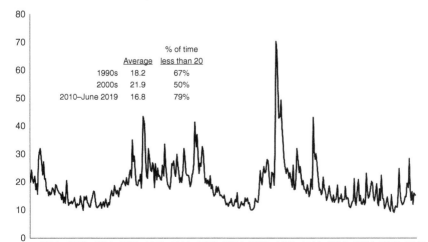

stock performance. In the 2010s, investors were chasing growth and momentum and free cash flow yielding companies underperformed the general market.

Is value investing dead?

The significant underperformance of value investing in the 2010s has led to a heated debate among professional investors on whether the entire concept of *value investing* is dead. Importantly, value investing in this debate is a fundamental company factor description. It is defined as owning the cheapest decile or quintile of stocks based on a price-to-book or P/E ratio. By this definition, value investing will again underperform in the 2020s. This is not because valuation no longer matters. *Valuation will always matter*. You cannot outperform the market buying overvalued stocks. However, there are reasons cheap stocks are underperforming, and those reasons are not going to change in the 2020s.

The most important reason for the underperformance of value stocks is that these stocks are in disrupted industries and industries will continue to be disrupted in the next decade. If you were to buy the bottom quintile of Russell 3000 stocks ranked by price-to-book ratio in December 2019, you would be significantly overweight the financial and energy sectors. The financial and energy sectors account for 53% of the cheapest stocks. If you think the world is going to mean revert to a place where established, traditional banks and oil-related companies are going to fundamentally outperform and lead the economy then you should own value stocks. Unfortunately, these industries are under major disruption and they will not mean revert as they did historically. The underperformance of financial and energy companies is not a cyclical issue, as it would have been historically. It is a disruption, paradigm shift issue.

The outperformance of cheap stocks historically was driven in part by it being better to buy cheap versus expensive, but also in large part due to cyclicality. Stocks are usually cheap at the bottom of economic cycles, so value investing was buying at the bottom of a business or industry cycle. That strategy is great as long as there is not a paradigm shift in the industry and cycles revert and reach higher highs. From 1930 to 2019, the US stock market has always rebounded to reach higher highs and recessions have averaged only 18 months. This cyclical upward trending environment was a key driver in the value factor outperforming from 1930 to 2019.

It may not be different forever, but value investing was different in the 2010s and will be different again in the 2020s. The financial sector is under stress from both increased regulation and technology. Earnings are, and will continue to be, pressured by increased regulation that has dictated lower leverage limits and high compliance. Banks cannot match their historic earnings power with 50% less leverage. While earnings are pressured by lower leverage, revenues are pressured by new competitors and a changing landscape. Physical branches and traditional payment mechanisms are facing a completely disrupted environment. ApplePay, Square, Libra, Venmo, Ally, and SoFi are just a few of the new competitors in the financial industry. Regardless of how cheap traditional banking stocks are, investors are taking a higher level of risk than they would have historically.

The energy complex and energy companies are under pressure from new technologies disrupting both the supply of energy and demand for energy. Supply is being affected by fracking technologies increasing production potential and lowering the cost of overall production. At the same time that supply is being economically increased in oil and natural gas fields, demand is being decreased as electric vehicles and ride sharing begin to take market share. Cheap energy stocks are much higher risk today than they ever were before.

There can be short-term, unexpected events that cause energy or banking companies to outperform for some period of time, but the risk of traditional companies being replaced is greater than ever before. Simplistically buying cheap stocks is not good enough to create outperformance in the foreseeable future.

To be completely clear, value investing underperforming in the 2020s does not mean valuation does not matter in making investment decisions. Buying good companies at reasonable or cheap valuations is very important. For active investment managers, understanding industries and selecting the best businesses are the two most important pursuits. The next section will focus on best practices in developing and executing on a repeatable, sustainable investment strategy and process that can create alpha.

CREATING ALPHA

Part II moves from the current environmental impacts on active investing to focus on executing a successful alpha-creating equity strategy. Investment managers must define a cohesive strategy and proactively execute a disciplined investment process. Only this combination of a cohesive strategy and disciplined execution can produce consistent, repeatable outperformance.

You must have long-range goals to keep you from being frustrated by short-range failures.

— *Charles C. Noble, US Army Major General*

Finding companies that will compound their earnings through superior business models is the key to outperformance. The market may ignore fundamental business performance for a period of time, but historically over a three-year period the market rarely has not compensated companies that produce results.

Alpha creation process and execution

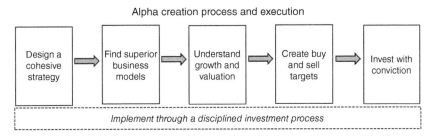

Implement through a disciplined investment process

As of January 1, 2010, there were 1,585 companies with a market cap over $250 million in the US, 205 (13%) are still public and produced a 20+% annualized return. There were another 300+ companies that were acquired and provided a 20% annualized return over at least three years. These are the companies that will drive outperformance for fund managers. On average, they consist of the top quintile in stock price return performance across the broad universe of US equities. This section is designed to help recognize long-term top quintile–performing companies and avoid companies that will dilute performance. Once companies are selected, managing the investments without making behavioral mistakes takes experience and a well-designed portfolio methodology.

CHAPTER 6

A COHESIVE STRATEGY

- *Aligning pieces of the puzzle*
- *Benchmarks and security universes that are too narrow or broad*
- *Diversification and performance goals*
- *Assets under management (AUM) relationship to the strategy*
- *Matching the time horizon of the strategy to the investor base*
- *Fees in relation to the strategy return potential*
- *Shorting and your strategy*
- *Academic analysis and investment reality*
- *Firm incentives*
- *Executing the strategy*

Before discussing the specific security selection and portfolio management keys to outperformance, managers need to understand both the potential and limitations of their strategy and define their firm goals. Many managers superficially address this important element of success, because they are so focused on other aspects of the fund. To achieve goals, they have to be well defined or execution and success will be impossible.

How much alpha do you expect and what type of volatility will you experience getting there?

This question often gets responses citing either overly optimistic hoped-for outcomes or recent performance trends. When questioned further many managers say, "We are going to do our best every day and our expertise will create good alpha over time." When asked to define "good," it is clear very little thought had ever gone into the question.

It is a very important question that has to be addressed to be successful. The answer has a lot of nuance to it. As an example, if a manager's strategy is to invest in long-only US equities with over a $5 billion market cap and maintain a high level of liquidity with a 50-name investment portfolio, they need to understand what level of alpha they can create. If they think they can produce 1,000 basis points of outperformance annually, they are simply wrong. It is not a judgment on the stock-picking ability or work ethic of the firm; the US large cap market is too efficient and 50 company holdings is too diversified to produce 1,000 basis points of outperformance over any meaningful time period.

Thinking about what level of outperformance is possible is an important exercise. Obviously every strategy is different and there will be a million different decision points, but it can be illuminating to look at a few back-of-the-envelope calculations. Figure 6.1 provides an analysis that shows the outperformance (excess return) of a broad universe of US stocks on a five-year rolling basis. The numbers are averages for the rolling five-year periods, but they do not vary widely by five-year period. Stocks in the first decile generally outperform by 25% and stocks in the tenth decile generally underperform by 26%.

If we had an equal-weight portfolio of 20 stocks and threw darts enough times, we would end up with 10% of the portfolio net asset value in each of the ten deciles (or two positions in each decile). The resulting return would be close to the average of the broad universe of US stocks. This assumes no behavioral mistakes in managing the portfolio or incredible trading strategies.

So what security selection success has to occur to achieve 1,000 basis points of alpha?

The necessary win-loss ratio is demonstrated in Figure 6.2. We would need to avoid deciles nine and ten completely, then we would have to have 85% of our portfolio or (17 of 20 names) in the top four deciles and 70% in the top three deciles (14 of 20 positions). This performance over five years would achieve 1,000 basis points of excess return annually over five years.

FIGURE 6.1   Five-year average rolling excess returns by decile 1998 to 2018; all US stocks greater than $500 million market cap–adjusted for inflation

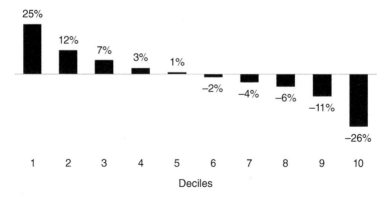

FIGURE 6.2   Five-year 1,000 bps excess return performance scenario

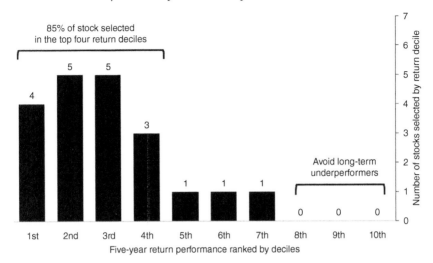

The point of the exercise is to recognize the difficulty of the task. In a concentrated portfolio, which is necessary to create significant outperformance, an investment manager must avoid all ninth and tenth decile–returning stocks. We will use 1,000 basis points of alpha as a goal or definition of success throughout in different exercises, but the fact is only the top decile of hedge fund managers reach this goal. Generally to reach 1,000 basis points of alpha some portion of a successful public equity hedge fund's alpha has to be created through portfolio management and a successful short portfolio. For a long-only manager with any volatility concerns, 500 basis points is a much more realistic strategic goal in liquid, developed markets. Although being more realistic, 500 basis points is still a goal that only a minority of managers will attain.

Aligning pieces of the puzzle

The following chart depicts the major pieces of the strategy puzzle needed to create repeatable outperformance and a sustainable firm. The investment activity pieces have to be put together to match your alpha goals and then you must have investors that are supportive of your strategy and understand your goals and limitations. No strategy can have everything, and sophisticated allocators are very aware of the balance that needs to be found in a fund strategy. Each manager must decide where return is prioritized over risk, concentration over diversification, and so on. Each piece of the puzzle is a balance and a decision about prioritization.

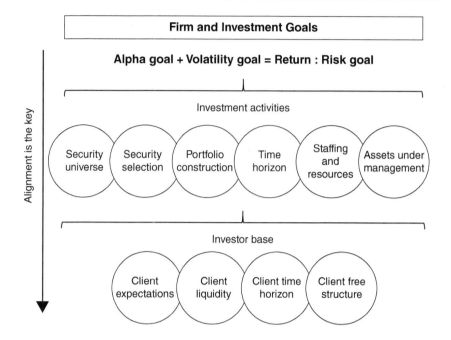

At Duke University Management Company (DUMAC), we see hundreds of hedge funds and long-only investment managers annually and listen to their pitches on why and how they will create outperformance and why they should be funded. The sheer number of managers looking for capital and the wide variety of strategies and execution methods is quite staggering. This discussion will focus on long-short equity hedge funds and long-only investment managers, but even within those two investment categories the execution of similar strategies can be very different. We have analyzed strategies, execution processes, and outcomes for more than 25 years, and there are clearly some strategies that do not work, some that are harder than others, some that are too expensive, and then there are some that *could* work. Cutting out the strategies where the pieces do not all fit together is often much easier than picking the winners from the remaining subset. Alignment of all the pieces to match the goals of the firm is the key.

Benchmarks and security selection universes that are too narrow or broad

Making a decision about the universe of companies you will focus your research on is incredibly important. The firm's universe of security selection options on an equally weighted basis should also be one of your internal benchmarks so that you can accurately perform security selection attribution without index weightings or other abnormalities distorting the analysis. This will most accurately judge security selection performance.

Some managers like to talk about absolute performance and don't like to think about a benchmark. Unfortunately, your investor base will have benchmarks and it is important to understand their expectations. An investment manager should not be a slave to a benchmark and be overly concerned about tracking error, but thinking you will not be graded based on a benchmark is naive. Benchmarks are not something anyone can avoid. Alpha is the risk-adjusted excess return over a benchmark, so you cannot create alpha without one. Capital allocators will have various benchmarks, and it is important to understand how they will analyze your returns in advance and discuss it. If you are a US long-only equity firm, you may be benchmarked to the S&P 500, but if your strategy would never buy a company with a market cap over $100 billion or never buy a financial sector company, you need your investor base to understand that in advance. If large caps and/or financials materially outperform, you may struggle for that period of time, even though your security selection and strategy in general may have performed very well compared to your actual universe.

Some managers choose an extremely narrow universe, because they are experienced in that area and see that as their edge. In fact, having an edge through experience or some other factor is very important. However, analysis needs to be done to make sure your universe is broad enough to achieve your return goals or you may have to change the other pieces of the strategy appropriately to compensate for a small security universe.

As an example, an experienced senior energy executive from Houston starting a fund focusing on US shale companies needs to consider that his universe is very highly correlated, because the public US energy exploration and production companies are at the whims of energy commodity prices. The total universe is approximately 100 companies. The subsector is highly volatile and can be in or out of favor at extremes for years. This creates a situation in which all that may matter is the level of balance sheet risk each company is taking. The companies may simply trade on their business leverage to the commodity price. Operational knowledge may not add the value one might expect. Being able to create consistent, repeatable outperformance through an operational knowledge edge in a 100-company, highly correlated and volatile universe, while trying to maintain even moderate liquidity or diversification, may be impossible. This is not due to the managers' lack of operational expertise but an understanding of what will and won't work in public markets. The strategy could be broadened in some way or the other pieces could be moved to try and extract everything possible out of the edge. A very concentrated (five to ten company) portfolio of micro and small cap energy companies would have a better chance of success, because you are allowing the very high portfolio concentration to overwhelm the high correlation of the sub-industry and using the more inefficient micro/small cap market to allow the edge to make a material difference. However, the other pieces have to fall in line. This new highly concentrated, small cap focus will have very low liquidity, need a very long time horizon, and be very volatile. The concentration and market cap change created the opportunity for outperformance, but it also created the opportunity for severe underperformance. The firm's investor base must understand the risks and have the same time horizon and volatility tolerance as the manager. Otherwise, allocators will pull their capital when underperformance occurs, potentially exiting at the worst time. Whether the manager was correct in his security selection does not matter at all, because he would be forced to sell at the worst time.

Too broad a universe is also problematic. It is hard to demonstrate an edge with a broad strategy, and special expertise is needed in many areas from academic background to language knowledge. In a broad universe the staffing and resources piece of the strategy would be important. The firm would have to be large and the leaders of the firm have to understand how to manage and motivate people, which is a different skill set from just being a good investor. It is all a balance, but the investment universe is an important issue that can hurt managers before they even get to pick their first stock.

Diversification and performance goals

Diversification is another key issue that will be fully developed in a later chapter on portfolio management (chapter 11). The primary diversification issue in determining a cohesive strategy is to understand what can be accomplished with different levels of portfolio concentration. The problems fall on both sides of the equation; some managers assume they can make much larger levels of alpha than is possible with a diversified portfolio, and some believe they can attain lower levels of volatility than is possible with a highly concentrated portfolio. As a rule of thumb, if the number of companies in your portfolio gets north of 8% of all the names in your universe you are not going to create high levels of alpha. As you move past the 15% of your universe threshold, you are creating more of a factor portfolio than an alpha-driven portfolio. Factor or more diversified portfolios can still produce alpha in the 0–200 basis points range, but not much beyond that level. Significant concentration is necessary to reach the 500–1,000 basis point outperformance level.

> *Don't screw up a perfectly good stock market strategy by diversifying your way into mediocre returns.*
>
> *—Joel Greenblatt, investor*

Many managers automatically state they will hold 20 to 25 names in their portfolio. When asked why, they cite Warren Buffett's theory on "de-worseification." Buffett is an investment genius and directionally his statement is true, but it's not that simple. A manager needs to think about concentration in relation to the specific universe. If you are an emerging markets manager with 5,000+ liquid companies, you can go higher than 25 companies and still gain benefits from diversification. Understanding your alpha goal and the correlations of the companies within your universe is the way to decide on the correct level of diversification. Focusing on a highly correlated sector will significantly shrink the number of companies that are optimal for diversification and alpha creation.

Assets under management (AUM) relationship to strategy

Matching the assets under management to your strategy is very important. There is a level of assets needed to achieve the personal financial goals of the manager and staff the firm. There is a level of assets optimal for creating alpha with the designed strategy. These two asset levels need to match in order for the manager and investors to both be happy.

This is one of the areas where goal congruence between manager and investor base can become a conflict. Analysis needs to be done to understand both sides of the equation. It is common for a manager's assets to outgrow firm strategy and for alpha to suffer from this strategy to asset mismatch. As great an investor as Warren Buffett is, an analysis of his early returns and more recent returns will demonstrate that the level of assets that Berkshire Hathaway now manages is simply not conducive to creating the outperformance produced in the early days of the firm. Understanding the designed strategy's AUM sweet spot is important. From a capital allocator's perspective, the sweet spot is the minimum level of assets needed to provide for the firm and keep talented people incentivized to perform. Obviously, an investment manager is looking to raise assets above this level to create personal wealth, hence the potential conflict.

Matching the time horizon of the strategy to the investor base

One of the toughest pieces to match is the strategy's time horizon to the investor base's time horizon. If managers think their strategy should produce results when viewed through a three-year time horizon lens and the investor states they analyze managers based on five years of performance then you have a match.

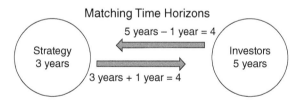

It is almost always the case that managers underestimate the time needed for their investment theses and strategy to play out and allocators always overestimate their willingness to be patient. A capital base that does not match the strategy's time horizon for successful investments is one of the biggest problems in the investment industry. Many good security selection ideas have been destroyed by having to sell before the thesis could play out. This is one of the key challenges to investing in today's central bank and disruption-driven markets. Time horizon is one of the most important tools that an active investor can use and if taken away it can make alpha creation impossible.

Fees in relation to the strategy return potential

There are often strategies managed by firms that may be successful on a gross basis, but at a level where the client's fees are not worth the returns created. Merger arbitrage is an example, because many merger arbitrage strategies can be created to demonstrate a high probability of an 8% return with low volatility, which is nice but you can't charge a 2% management fee and 20% carry on an 8% gross return strategy. There are simpler and less market-directional ways to get that anticipated net return. Managers should think about fees in relation to their alpha goals. Estimating what percentage of alpha will be earned by the manager and what percentage will be kept by the allocator can be an enlightening exercise. If a manager is most likely going to keep 80% of the alpha created due to the fee structure, why would the investor base be happy with a 20% share? The best relationships in any business are win-win, so fee structure should evidence this goal.

Shorting and your strategy

For hedge fund managers shorting is a big part of the overall strategy and has to be used to both create value and, you hope, to enhance decision-making on the long side of the portfolio. The one thing shorting is *not* is the opposite methodology of the long-only process. Of course, you would like to short companies that do not meet your long security selection process, but it is not that simple. There are definable, quantifiable reasons why constructing and managing your short portfolio in the mirror opposite way of your long portfolio is a losing strategy. This will be discussed in detail in the chapter on short investing (chapter 12). A manager must understand the goals, potential, and limitations of their short strategy and how it fits in the overall portfolio.

Academic analysis and investment reality

Many strategies are designed from academic research and historic backtesting. Backtesting strategies can be interesting and a good learning process, but there are a number of reasons why it is very different from investing reality.

The first reason is that public market security investment data are very limited. Liquid public market investing is actually a very recent activity. Basic data can go back to 1950, but most data are only robust back to 1980 or 1990. Before 1980, financial data are very scarce due to the lack of computers. There was not even an emerging markets index before 1987. Twenty or thirty years is a very short period of time in relation to business history, so putting a high degree of faith in 30 years of backtesting is not robust enough. As an example, since the new millennium, interest rates have been on a powerful downward trend, so all data have been influenced by this specific rate environment. One can also think of the data in economic business cycle terms. If there are 20 or 30 years of data, the strategy is being tested through three or four economic cycles; not very robust.

The second reason is that academic research on strategies have a time horizon that is totally unpressured. A strategy may look great over a 20-year period, but the academics did not have to go through the three-year period of negative returns shown in the analysis. In reviewing academic research, the three years of negative returns look like a brief drop in the graph that is otherwise positive. The actual reality is that the brief three-year drop could have caused behavioral mistakes, investor outflows, or potential loss of conviction in the strategy itself. The backtest cannot feel the stress of that period. An investor could never know everything works out well in the end for the strategy, so they may make strategy changes that are harmful.

As we will discuss in more detail later, investing is as much psychological, as quantitative. Scientific and academic research is unable to capture the stress of investing reality. Strategies should have foundations in economic principle and backtests should be interesting anecdotal examples that may influence ideas, but not be relied on as scientific truth.

Firm incentives

Incentives are important in any organization and hedge funds are no exception. Capital allocators enjoy goal congruence with hedge fund managers through a carry-driven compensation relationship. *Carry* is the incentive fee earned by investment managers based on the returns to their clients. The strategy and historic success of different hedge funds demand different levels of carry from their client base. The incentive fee can range from a few percentage points over a benchmark to 20%, or even 30%, of the absolute returns of the fund. It is important for this goal congruence with clients to be shared across the firm with investment professionals at every level. Hedge funds have been successful with a variety of employee incentive structures. They range from completely team-oriented bonus structures shared equally to very individualistic structures, in which analysts are compensated only on the success of the portfolio companies they specifically work on and have convinced the portfolio manager to place in the portfolio.

From my experience, the firm-incentive compensation structure is often reflective of the personality of the portfolio manager or fund owner. Although there is no correct answer, the key is, again, alignment with the other pieces of the strategy and an understanding of the implications. If the firm is founded on a buy-and-hold, long-term, equity-investing philosophy, purely individualistic return-oriented compensation (termed *eat what you kill* on Wall Street) is not a great match. It will create shorter-term decisions by analysts trying to maximize their annual bonus. Generally the more focus put on annual return-driven, individually directed bonuses, the higher both the portfolio trading turnover and the employee turnover will be at the firm. On the other end of the spectrum is a complete team approach, in which everyone is compensated at the same level. This approach has the disadvantage of not forcing employees to feel responsibility for their specific work, and often top performers will feel undercompensated and leave the firm.

For an investment firm with longer-term investment time horizons and goals of building a sustainable, stable organization, I recommend a mix of both team and individual incentives executed by both quantitative and qualitative decisions. If a bonus pool for all employees is created and calculated based on the firm's success over a period of time that is influenced by the time horizon of firm investments, the goal congruence of employee, firm, and client has been established. A firm's investment time horizon may be five or ten years, which is probably not realistic for many employees, so three years is a fair compromise. Once the bonus pool is created quantitatively, qualitative assessment by the portfolio manager/founder(s) is the best way to distribute incentive compensation.

Qualitative decision-making at this point is necessary to recognize employees who may have worked on longer-term projects with no direct financial gain, such as process technologies or future relationships. It can also be used to balance outcomes that may be more luck than good judgment and work. The profession of investing has a healthy dose of luck in determining success, even over intermediate time periods. Employees who happen to pick a hot sector or stock should not be overly compensated or it sends the wrong message to the organization. These compensation decisions have to be qualitative, because there are simply too many scenarios to account for quantitatively. The idea of quantitative compensation decision-making often creates an expectation for a higher level of fairness and less friction in inter-firm relationships, but generally this is more of an illusion than reality. At the end of the day, managers in any organization are paid to make good decisions and compensation issues cannot be an exception for portfolio managers. Importantly, managers need to be very transparent and predictable on how they will make qualitative compensation decisions, so analysts understand expectations and can generally be prepared for outcomes. The hedge fund industry has always been very competitive and compensation is both high and often volatile, so transparency, honesty, empathy, and predictability in decisions will aid in long-term success.

There is no question incentive structures are key to the culture, success, and strategy of the firm and should be given a lot of thought by fund managers before being implemented.

Executing the strategy

Last, it is surprising that some managers simply do not execute on their strategy and once funded go far afield from their initial presentations to investors. Sometimes this is poor process, but sometimes it is a belief by managers that they were funded to make money and they can go about it however they want. Both of these are poor decisions. A business would never try to operate without an operational strategy; why would an investment firm work that way? Without defining and implementing a disciplined strategy, it is very hard to be successful in an already difficult profession. If you are an emerging market small cap manager funded based on your deep due diligence networks in China, don't buy Microsoft because you heard it was a good idea from another successful hedge fund manager. It may be a great idea for that manager, but for you it is *style shift,* which is the act of changing a strategy, because it is not working or the manager is undisciplined. When managers shift their style of investing there is an above-average chance they will fail. Professional allocators of capital watch their managers closely for these signs of a lack of conviction in how capital is being invested.

Managing money for clients means executing on the strategy that they funded in order to meet their investment goals. An integral part of executing on a defined strategy is putting in place a solid investment process. Once a cohesive strategy is put in place, the day-to-day work of a successful manager is in the investment process designed on fundamental analysis and research due diligence.

CHAPTER 7

INVESTMENT PROCESS

- *Process evolves; it is not stagnant*
- *Functions served by process*
- *Documenting and memory*
- *Investment thesis*
- *Deep work: Trying to avoid the noise*
- *Channel checks*
- *Management meetings*
- *Systems and technology*

Process is the keystone to a good investment firm, whether it be a hedge fund, long-only equity or credit fund, endowment, or family office. Process is what allows you to analyze and understand your mistakes and successes and learn. Without it, you will make the same mistakes over and over and often won't know when you have made a mistake. The financial markets are not like science or math where you have discoveries and they are determined to be truths. A 70% win rate is great. In most professional jobs, if you are wrong 30% of the time it is cause to be fired.

Even more confounding is that you can win for the wrong reasons and lose for the right reasons. The same decision can look great or terrible at different time intervals. Your goal in being a good investor is to create a repeatable, sustainable process. Anyone can randomly buy hot stocks and look great for a period of time, but it won't be sustainable. A detailed process at every step is what enables an investor to historically analyze decisions and try to improve them in the future. The process will be a reflection of the investor's core beliefs and investment tenets The creation of the process will force the investor to think deeply about these important issues. Investment tenets are nuanced and have to be deeply considered to create conviction during times of stress. As an example, one can cite being a contrarian as a key tenet, but that can mean so many different things under different scenarios and in different environments.

Process has to be built for both security selection and portfolio management. Some firms founded by experienced portfolio managers design process on security selection, but leave portfolio management up to the experienced founder to handle on his or her own. Portfolio managers or CIOs, no matter how experienced, should still hold themselves to communicating how they expect to make decisions and then recording their actions for later analysis. The belief that when only one person is involved in certain decisions, there is no need for process is wrong. The articulation of process will help that person learn and allow others to add value.

Process evolves; it is not stagnant

Importantly, process does not mean stagnation. An investment process should change, adapt, and evolve. If it is not evolving the investor is not learning. The process does have to be stable enough to analyze outcomes well, but when those outcomes provide new insights the process should change. Good detailed process should lead to the frequent analysis of decisions, which should provide insights into enhancing the process.

Trial and error is also a part of an evolving process. An investment process has an extensive list of due diligence and analysis tasks. Adding a new task to a process is about learning and should be done with the very open understanding that it may or may not add value and should be monitored. You have to continually assess the value of each step that is being taken in relation to other activities, such as firm resources or time spent on current positions relative to new idea generation. Adding new tasks to an investment process creates new questions and leads to viewing decisions from different perspectives. In the end, even new tasks that later are deemed too time-consuming and deleted from the process have added value through learning and trying new things.

Process is also not about putting handcuffs on decision-makers; there are times when a portfolio manager or CIO may want to break a defined process. That may be the right decision, but record and recognize that the process was broken for this unique scenario and try to learn from that scenario. Unique situations do arise and common sense says do not be a slave to any process.

Functions served by process

Process serves a number of important functions, not simply due diligence. Some of the primary advantages from a disciplined process are highlighted here:

- **Firm beliefs and conviction.** Having a well-thought-out process and core investment tenets is integral to understanding why you make decisions and guides the firm. It forces introspection.
- **Focus.** By thinking deeply about how you want to do things, not just about the current company in your portfolio, you will focus your actions and time in the right direction. You will disseminate data to find the important pieces that add value to your decisions.

- **Repeatability.** Nothing can be repeated that was not clearly defined initially. As an example, due diligence checklists ensure things are not being forgotten, and management interview checklists create a baseline for discussions.
- **Staff management.** Process enables a firm to grow and bring on new talented people. If new hires are brought into a firm with no process or beliefs, they cannot be trained on what has been learned to date. It is hoped that with a clear investment process in place, they will learn and enhance the process.
- **Behavioral stability.** Process helps avoid behavioral mistakes, which will be discussed in more detail in the chapter on portfolio management (chapter 11). Under stressful situations, if you have previously thought about how you will handle stressful events it will aid in your making the best decision.
- **Historical analysis of decisions.** Without good data on what was done historically, you cannot analyze decisions and learn. Attribution and case studies on your decisions is paramount to a successful firm, so you must have good data.

> *One thing that could help would be to write down the reason you are buying a stock before your purchase. Write down "I am buying Microsoft at $300 billion because ... " Force yourself to write this down. It clarifies your mind and discipline.*
>
> —*Warren Buffett, investor*

Documenting and memory

There are many important process practices, including due diligence checklists, channel checks, timely management meetings, and more, but the act of recording and documenting is central to all of them. Recording research notes, decision points, and a final investment thesis has to be done to perform accurate analysis, create conviction, and involve people throughout the firm. Humans are irrational and they misremember (significantly).

We not only forget things, but also we misremember reality; everyone does. There are close to a hundred different memory biases that psychologists have documented. A memory bias is enhancing or impairing the recall of a memory. Some of the key memory biases in relation to investing are as follows:

- **Consistency bias.** Remembering one's past attitudes or opinions as resembling your current opinion. As an example, you may remember the stock that doubled last year as always having been your favorite.
- **Mood and stress congruent bias.** The relationship between your memory and the effect of mood and stress. Combined with consistency bias, an example would be when a portfolio manager had a bad night and comes into work in the morning to find a portfolio company has missed earnings and is down 15%. The manager sells all the stock in a rush saying he or she had always hated that stock.

- **Confirmation bias.** Our tendency is to like to talk to those who have the same beliefs and to interpret information in a way that conforms to our beliefs. Many of the most successful investors go out of their way to listen to those with different opinions and encourage other firm members to try and produce evidence that might poke holes in their investment thesis.
- **Choice supportive bias.** Remembering the path taken as having been the best option and failing to recall those paths that were rejected along the way. Opportunity costs associated with investment decision-making are often hard to quantify but are very meaningful.
- **Hindsight bias.** The tendency to see past events as being predictable. After an event has occurred, you may incorrectly convince yourself that you had seen that coming all along.
- **Egocentric and self-serving biases.** Quite similar biases, egocentricity causes you to recall the past in a self-serving manner, and self-serving bias causes you to perceive yourself responsible for successes and not responsible for failures. Remembering it was you who made a great investment call to buy Nike at $35, now that it is $60, when in fact it was a team decision and you bought Nike at $60 initially and then again at $35, so really you averaged in at about $47, but you just remember the $35 trade.
- **Rosy perception bias.** Remembering the past as better than it actually was. The concept of nostalgia is rooted in the rosy perception bias, such as remembering the 1990s as a time of prosperity and lack of conflict, when in fact there were as many ups and downs as any other decade.
- **Peak-end bias.** People often remember the peak of an event as opposed to the average or sum total of the experience. Remembering a past trade in a very positive manner, because the company was bought out at a 25% premium, when actually it was a frustrating three-year investment that finally got bought out at the initial purchase price.

There are more than 100 different memory biases, but let's hope these examples have convinced you that to find truth and make accurate assessments of your decision process, you have to write things down and keep records. From an initial research perspective, this documentation culminates in an *investment thesis,* which should highlight all the reasons you are involved in a company and all the concerns you have that should be monitored.

Investment thesis

The investment thesis is unique for every company. However, there are some issues that are common across all investments and should be addressed in every investment thesis. Sales expectations should be specifically addressed over the next three years and generally addressed over longer time periods. Expectations have to be very detailed and thorough. It is of little value to write "the company should have solid sales growth"; your memory biases are going to read that as 4% sales growth three years later, because that's what they achieved, when in fact you were thinking 8% sales growth in your initial due diligence. Even when citing that you expect 8% sales growth, it is best to detail from which products or divisions you expect growth to come from. Industry sales expectations and market share should also be noted; potentially the company underperforms expectations but is taking market share at a greater pace than expected.

Margin expectations are always a focus. Gross margins and operating margins should be detailed separately. If gross margin improvement of 50 bps per year is expected, define why that improvement is expected to occur, so you are not fooled by other factors that may be transient in nature affecting margins. The most important metric in the cost structure of many companies is usually a marketing cost metric. The key metric may be customer acquisition cost, sales staff productivity, or some other sales to marketing relationship. Being very detailed about how the metric will evolve helps track trends over time.

There are many other financial ratios and metrics that can be followed based on the specific company. One key focus of the investment thesis should be specific research that needs to be done in order to track the successes and failures of the company. This can include specific channel checks, industry data, management questions that should always be asked, or competitor activities. The point is to provide focus for determining if the investment is proceeding as expected. Creating a detailed list of concerns to monitor is a part of every investment thesis. In summary, the investment thesis should define both expectations and methods to track those expectations throughout the investment.

Another documentation tool that can be helpful is to keep an investment diary. Spending a few minutes each day or an hour at the end of the week to record your thoughts and what you were working on can be very informative. For reading and writing learners there is also a benefit to your memory and thought process in the act of writing. In addition to learning about your thought process and the decisions you made, maintaining an investment diary can help with time management. With the endless amount of research that can be done in pursuit of investment research time management is very important to success. As you write down what you accomplished during the week, you may realize that you are continually spending time on a subject or task that is not productive in creating investment returns. Can you avoid or delegate certain activities to spend more time on research that may make a difference in returns?

In your process, you will create financial projection models, and they will evolve and change over time as results come in and new research is done. It is informative to keep versions of the financial models and be able to go back and look at what your projections were at the time you initially entered the investment. It is very common to own a stock for two or three years in a good market and have the stock increase in price by 20%, but when you go back and look at the initial financial projections you realize that the company has not achieved your original expectations. That is winning when you were wrong. The market did all the work for you. This might be a good investment position to sell now. When the market does pull back and your stock drops 20%, you do not want to be stuck with an investment that has fundamentally underperformed and falls into the behavioral trap of "well it is cheap now, so let's hold on longer." A company that underperforms consistently in a good environment is cheap for a reason.

> *I believe that good investors are successful not because of their IQ, but because they have an investing discipline.*
> —*Stanley Druckenmiller, investor*

Deep work: Trying to avoid the noise

There is probably no other industry inundated with as much extraneous, unimportant data produced by traditional media outlets, social media, research houses, technical chartists, and the list goes on. Additionally, your portfolio continuously moves all day. You are rightly concerned with your performance, so, of course, you should check the markets routinely. However, constant checking of inconsequential price moves throughout the day can be a problem. In the investment business it is very possible to spend all day monitoring macro news flow and watching the stock prices of your portfolio holdings move up and down. At the end of the day, step back and think about what you accomplished from a real company research perspective.

> *Research will take some work. The good news is that you will be well paid.*
> —*Joel Greenblatt*

Are you spending too much time watching stock prices bounce back and forth? Process and self-assessment are the only way to stop yourself going down the rabbit hole of daily stock action and extraneous news flow. The fact is the first half-hour of the day probably tells you which stocks are moving materially and then, maybe you need to check in one or two times during the day. If you are not a trader, there is no reason to check every half-hour and have prices streaming across your monitors. Successful fundamental investors need to spend time on original research and deep understanding of companies and industries. Focusing on process helps avoid wasting time on market noise. This one issue can make a big difference in time management, the culture of the firm, and overall success.

Channel checks

One way to potentially get yourself away from the price monitors and superficial news is to put extra focus on channel checks. Channel checks are a great way to understand industries and get inside the company in which you are invested.

Channel checks can come in many forms, from hour-long conversations with experts in an industry to calling individual retail stores to ask about branded product sales. Customers, suppliers, competitors, and consultants are primary channel check candidates. Attending industry conferences offers the opportunity to talk to company competitors and understand how the companies in the industry position themselves from a marketing perspective. Attending an industry conference for the first time is very helpful, but doesn't always give you the full perspective that attending a conference many years in a row will offer. Over years you can create relationships and see how the industry is evolving and the different issues that arise as focal points each year.

> *As a general rule, the most successful man in life is the man who has the best information.*
> —Benjamin Disraeli, UK Prime Minister

It is often the case that financial analysts are not the best channel check interviewers in the firm. A research journalist or someone with a similar type of background can often solicit the best information. The ability to interview someone who probably has no real reason to talk to you and engage that person in conversation and have him or her open up about business issues is a unique talent. Some financial analysts are not suited to it, so that is why you want a team with diverse skill sets.

Information is an advantage. Many people think they have to have unique information that no one else can get, but often it is simply that you may know what the information means while others do not. The information may also be readily accessible, but others did not bother to ask and you did. Channel checks are also driven by the specific expectations and concerns stated in the investment thesis. This all takes time and effort, but is the best path to a repeatable and sustainable outperformance.

> *Most people won't put in the time to get a knowledge advantage.*
> —Warren Buffett, investor

Information discussions now often lead to the subject of alternative data and how it can be best used. There are many providers of alternative data offering information on everything from the weather to the number of cars in a parking lot to product inventory web scraping to railroad car tracking. The amount of data is pretty staggering and will continue to expand. The most important thing to a fundamental investor is to understand what your investment thesis is and whether these specific data actually have any bearing on the issues in the investment thesis and your company. It is interesting to know that there will be a snowstorm on Black Friday in the Midwest and retailers might have trouble getting people to their stores, but is it really important to your company's investment thesis? Alternative data is very often short term in nature, so it may lend itself more to decisions about the short side of the portfolio.

Alternative data will most likely not revolutionize the investment research process, but there is no reason not to investigate different offerings and try to understand whether the data may fit into your process at different times.

Management meetings

In order to have a clear vision of the company and create a detailed investment thesis, meetings with company executives are part of any good due diligence process. Many management meetings are arranged at sell-side (investment bank) conferences in major financial center cities around the world. This is great for initial meetings, but once you have decided you are truly interested in a company it is best to travel to the company headquarters. At sell-side conferences, CEOs and CFOs are having eight to ten 45-minute meetings a day with different investors and reciting the same story over and over again. There is a pretty good chance they may not remember you a week later. When you take the time to travel to small and mid-tier cities and take site tours, the management teams remember you. You get much more detailed answers and they will take your phone call in the future regardless of how large a shareholder you are at the moment. They will make sure they make time for you at future sell-side conferences and be willing to listen to your input. Everyone knows, the human capital of a company is as important as financial capital, but making an assessment of management and their ability to execute on their strategy is one of the toughest parts of due diligence. Meeting management in their offices aids exponentially in the process.

When meeting with company management, you have to be prepared. Just walking in the door and letting the chief financial officer (CFO) speak for an hour is not that productive. Setting up management meetings is time-consuming and logistically difficult, so you need to make the most out of each meeting. A process for how to prepare and what types of questions you ask is very helpful. Prepare by reading all the latest releases and your past notes. There is no reason to waste time having the CFO tell you something that you could have read in the latest release. Management meetings should center on issues that were not specifically addressed publicly recently or on the whys of what was released recently. Asking, "What has been the trend in operating margins lately?" is less productive, because you can analyze the trend from the financial statements. Ask *why* operating margins have improved by 50 basis points and go on from there. If you discussed the different factors affecting margins in a June meeting, review your notes before your October meeting. Ask the same question and be prepared to remind the management team of their answer four months ago. This will allow a deeper understanding and provide an indication of whether things are progressing with the business in the way you expected.

Being confrontational with management teams is rarely productive, but tough questions have to be asked and company executives are fiduciaries of shareholder capital and should understand that responsibility. In asking tough questions there may be times that CFOs balk and cite regulation FD (fair disclosure laws) as a reason they cannot answer fully. That may be true and is a CFO's legal responsibility, but that is the CFO's line to draw around certain questions. You cannot know exactly which questions the CFO will consider over the line, so ask and let the CFO draw the line. If there are questions the CFO cannot answer try to rephrase them so that they might be able to answer. It is also often productive to share some of your peer group and industry expert channel check research with management to dig deeper into issues. If your channel checks on a new software release are indicating disgruntled customers due to compatibility or a service issue, then let the CFO know that you have been hearing this and get their feedback. Company executives are usually very interested in your channel check research. How they handle concerns or criticisms can also aid in management assessments.

Systems and technology

Recording of research and decisions is a top priority, but it is very time-consuming. It can become so overwhelming that you get bogged down and do not take good notes or don't review your notes when you make decisions due to difficulty finding them or the time it will take to review. You have to continually try new methods to make taking notes incredibly simple and the ability to review those notes simple with fast access. Even small things such as opening different software packages to do certain process tasks that are not used for other tasks creates too much friction. If you always have Bloomberg and Excel up all day every day, taking notes in a word processing software in different files may be too cumbersome. Will you open the software, dig through directories, and open all the separate files that were created over the years to review notes? Record keeping is of no use if you do not access and review the notes. Experiment with many different technology aids and find a way to document in the most efficient fashion.

Investment process is not just for large firms with many analysts; small firms can benefit just as much. Spending time on creating the right investment process for a firm will help with time management, research quality, attribution analysis, and developing the firm culture.

Artificial intelligence and natural language recognition software is becoming prevalent in the mining of data and sifting through the incredible flow of daily information. It has an important place in this type of investment support, because providing faster and better organized data points to an investment firm is an advantage. It will, however, be a very long time before technology is outperforming human investment decision-makers, because there is still as much art as science in a successful process, as we will further discuss in the chapters on valuation (chapter 9) and portfolio management (chapter 11).

CHAPTER 8

SECURITY SELECTION

- *Superior business models*
- *Idea generation: Top down to narrow the universe*
- *Timing business cycles*
- *Roll-up acquisition strategy*
- *Other types of companies to be wary of*
- *What to look for in a company: Sales growth*
- *What to look for in a company: Operating margins*
- *What to look for in a company: Market power sustainability*
- *Management teams*
- *Being contrarian and time horizon*

At its core fundamental investing is about a business and its ability to create cash flow in that moment and in the future. That statement is very simple and complex at the same time, because there are hundreds of data points and analyses that go into trying to determine if you are investing in a business that will create your forecasted cash flows even in a "research vacuum."

A research vacuum is a purely fictional place where you only get the facts that may pertain to your investment and nothing else. Because a research vacuum does not exist, an already complex decision is compounded when the actual decision data points are inter-mixed with millions of potentially irrelevant data points from hundreds of sources. This constant flow of financial data, industry news, global news, alternative data, pundit and peer opinions, Wall Street recommendations, channel checks, macro analysis, tweets, and technical analysis are all the potential pieces to an investment puzzle. You are trying to put your chosen puzzle together from the pieces of a hundred different puzzles and lots of random confetti intermixed. The fundamental research process is finding the pieces to your chosen puzzle from the massive pile of data pieces and trying to put it together to formulate an opinion. Once you start to see your puzzle take shape, you must decide whether you want to keep working on that puzzle or you should be starting a different one, because the original puzzle was not turning out to be a compelling opportunity. This is all in the hope of piecing together those few investment puzzles that will provide superior returns and, you hope, drive outperformance for years.

> *Behind every stock is a company. Find out what it's doing.*
> —*Peter Lynch, investor*

So focus and cutting through the irrelevant data of the day becomes a key skill set of the active investor and speaks to chapter 7 on process. Fundamental investing focuses on a company: the asset base, customers, competitive advantages, future strategies, capital allocation, and the business model. The analysis is to determine if that company will create better cash flows in the future than they do today and (importantly) if those future cash flows are not already discounted into the current market valuation.

There are many ways to use fundamental investing for different risk/return outcomes; it can be used for creating diversified portfolios that aim to produce alpha in the range of 0–400 basis points. It can be used to create both long and short portfolios or to create relative value trades that create alpha with low volatility, and it can be used in a concentrated portfolio. For the rest of these chapters, we will focus on the concentrated strategy with the goal of producing greater than 1,000 basis points in a sustainable manner annually. The same concepts can always be used in a more diluted format to lower volatility to a desired degree, but of course, superior returns will dissipate as diversification increases. *Risk and return characteristics are goals defined in a strategy and determined by portfolio construction, but core security selection crosses all equity strategies regardless of how the portfolio is constructed.*

Superior business models

In the next chapter we will discuss valuation, which is an important part of performance, but valuation is secondary to finding companies with superior business models. Investing on valuation alone will lead to being involved with weak companies or finding interesting trading ideas, but valuation will not recognize the long-term investments that will create outperformance over years.

> *I believe that the greatest long-range investment profits are never obtained by investing in marginal companies.*
> —*Philip Fisher, investor*

We will focus on identifying companies that we might be able to hold for a decade and avoiding those that will not have the ability to be long-term outperformers. Our initial time horizon won't be a decade, because it would be an unrealistic time horizon, but selecting companies that may have the ability to be decade-long investments is the goal. In analyzing hundreds and hundreds of hedge funds, the ability to find these decade long outperformers is evident in success. Outperformance for a decade demands executing on a business strategy that has a path to growth and a solid return on equity proposition. The ability to grow revenues has to be the first building block in the search. A company that cannot grow revenues above GDP growth will never be a *long-term* outperformer.

Recognizing companies with long-term superior business models is more difficult than understanding valuation, because cash flows are quantifiable and identified in accounting statements. Superior business models are recognized by understanding products, industries, and competitive positioning. A large part of the search for superior business models is pattern recognition from business models that have been successful in the past.

- What types of metrics have demonstrated superior business models in the past?
- What types of companies are more apt to have sustainable high returns on equity?
- What types of companies can be quickly deleted from the search?

Idea generation: Top down to narrow the universe

Idea generation can be both top down and bottom up. A combination that fits your strategy is the best answer. Often top-down firm-wide screening can be productive to begin the process. We have talked about the incredible amount of data in the investment business and to that point, it can be very productive to first decide what you don't want to invest in.

Using all US companies over $500 million in market cap as an example, the universe is about 3,000 companies with as many as 15% of the companies that should be actively avoided. You could also have another 15% that generally should be avoided unless there are catalysts or economic cycle events that you feel very confident will occur.

Removing companies from the search process is helpful from a time management perspective, but it is also helpful to think through the types of characteristics that are not conducive to creating long-term outperformance.

- **Heavily regulated companies.** Companies that have been granted a non-cyclical monopolistic asset should at best only return the cost of capital over time. Their financial statements will be an open book to the regulators and if they start to make an above-market rate of return, the regulators are going to change the rules and knock the return back down. Companies that fall into this category generally are utilities, toll roads, and other major infrastructure projects. They could increase their returns by using excess leverage to boost original projections, but that will make them even more interest rate sensitive than they already are, and an investor is still getting the same return per unit of risk. It would be better to buy non-overly levered, better-managed utilities and lever them yourself through portfolio balance sheet margin. There may also be intermediate term windows of time, where specific events push their valuations below the cost of capital, usually due to market concerns over extensions of licenses or change in regulation. In emerging markets, regulated companies are commonly raided for cash in a change of political administrations, especially those with a populist bias. This is particularly bad, because you accept an average equity cost of capital return and then every five or six years lose 20% on political regulation changes.

In the 2010s, central bank intervention and global low rates have been a great stimulant to the utility sector returns. Utilities have added significant leverage to their balance sheets, yet still rarely reach top quintile (deciles one or two) in historic return performance analysis. The only utility or toll road companies that reached the top quintile in the five-year annual rolling performance analysis were emerging market utilities, where prior underperformance was the key in a strong five-year return period. Nothing is absolute in investing, as there were two US water utility companies (of 300 companies in total) in the 2019 top returning quintile, but generally you can avoid these regulated companies and take 5% of the overall universe off your research list.

- **Companies you don't have the knowledge base to invest in.** Biotech is a simple example and many managers delete biotech companies from their internal universe. There is too much scientific specific knowledge needed combined with large binary events for most investors to be productive. Given this need for specialty knowledge and avoidance by most deep research fund managers, it can be a very good focus area for a small subset of managers with both scientific and investment management expertise. The biotech and small pharma subsector will produce companies that achieve long-term returns in the top quintile, but they will also produce even more bottom-quintile-return companies. Without specific expertise, the subsector is too much risk to warrant the time. This group accounts for about 5% of companies. Remember, the ability to create significant outperformance is very difficult to achieve if some portfolio holdings fall into the ninth and tenth deciles of return performance.

> If you don't feel comfortable making a rough estimate of the asset's future earnings, just forget it and move on.
>
> —*Warren Buffett, investor*

The exact companies are specific to each investment manager, but there are probably another 3% of the US company universe in earlier stage, very high scientific technology companies, where you may not have the expertise to invest without too much risk. These companies will also have a wide range of outcomes with a few in the top quintile of returns, but even more in the bottom quintile. This is another group of companies it would be best to avoid, unless you have very high conviction in your ability to be correct.

- **Sum-of-the-parts stories.** Many managers like sum-of-the-parts investment opportunities, investments in which when each part of a company is valued separately and the parts are added up, the total is worth materially more than the current market price. I have heard hundreds of pitches with sum-of-the-parts as the foundation of the investment thesis. My experience personally, and in watching many managers over a long time, is that they rarely work the way expected.

As an example, a company has a $400 million market cap and trades at $6 a share. It produces a product that was really hot five years ago, but lost demand and sales have been dropping about 5% per year and operating margins are doing the same. They are cutting staff to try and maintain margins and stay cash flow break even. They have $3 per share in net cash, own an office building worth $4 per share, and they are incubating a young new business that has potential. It's a free option, because the cash and office building are worth more than the current stock price! I would estimate one in ten of these opportunities make an above-market return. They will certainly not be decade-long compounders and will eat up research time and portfolio exposure. There are a number of reasons sum-of-the-parts opportunities fail. The most common reason is management has no interest in breaking up the company to realize shareholder value, because they would be firing themselves. Often the company is their personal identity, because they are founders or friends and family of the founders. There is the additional likelihood that management is poor, hence the reason for declining sales, margins, and low valuation. This management often succumbs to the allure of growth and redirects cash flow into risky projects to try and reestablish the past glory of the company,

- **Dying industries/distressed companies.** Some firms have expertise in distressed company investing, which can be a great strategy. However, if you don't have this specific expertise, this is another group to avoid. Heavily distressed and dying industry companies can achieve great one- or two-year returns, but compounding over five and ten years is not going to happen. There is some qualitative decision-making in creating this group, but it generally will account for about 2% of the universe. Although there will be a few big winners in one- and two-year periods, the vast majority of these companies will produce five- and ten-year returns in the bottom half of the universe. It is important to make a realistic decision on whether your firm has the expertise to tackle distressed company opportunities.

- **Small regional banks.** Small regional bank investments have all of the traits just mentioned. They are part of a disrupted industry without the capital to compete in creating new financial technologies to keep up with change. They are, also, regulated and take some specific expertise to understand. There is an M&A thesis about small banks being bought by bigger banks that has slowly played out since the new millennium, but return on equity is generally low and there is generally very little growth. The combination of all these factors makes it a very easy group of companies to pass on.

If you combine heavily regulated companies, companies with the necessity for very high levels of technological expertise, sum-of-the-parts stories, dying industries, and small regional banks, the universe of companies can be cut down by over 15%. This top-down analysis both saves time and provides focus to the research process.

> *If you buy the same securities everyone else is buying, you will have the same results as everyone else.*
>
> —*Sir John Templeton, investor*

Timing business cycles

There is another subset of companies, where above-average returns can be made, but you have to forecast a major industry shift or event within a certain time horizon. Every company is affected by cycles, but these are the companies that have high volatility in their sales growth and operating margins during different parts of the business cycle. These companies will not make top quintile returns through a cycle, so a major part of investing in these companies is being correct about where you are in the current industry cycle. *This is precisely the type of investment that has been most affected by the low rates and disruption of the last decade, so be wary of assuming historic trends are predictive of the future.*

If a manager does have some portion of the portfolio invested in these types of cyclical companies, they must be managed differently than long-term compounders from both a research and portfolio perspective. From a research perspective recognizing that the specific industry is more important than individual company selection is the first step. Companies in this group will be highly correlated and will not be able to outperform in a down cycle. You can pick the best of the group, but in a down cycle that will not add much value. One of the more important issues in highly cyclical security selection is balance sheet analysis to determine if the company you are investing in has the ability to sustain the down cycle. In an up cycle, the more highly levered companies often bounce back the most and can be very strong performers. The focus should be the cycle and how the industry manages the cycle. Here are some questions that need to be answered:

- How much will demand drop in the down cycle?
- How much capex was spent in the industry creating new supply capacity during the up cycle?
- Is there rational competition in the industry?
- Will some players go bankrupt consolidating the industry?

Companies in this highly cyclical group include energy exploration and production, oil service, auto-related, shipping, materials, and similar companies with commodity pricing and capex intensity. Many of these companies will drop customer prices to below economic levels during a down cycle, because marginal cash costs are all that matter. The goal is to survive the down cycle, not provide shareholders a reasonable return on capital. Digging in and understanding the volatility of the company cash flows and trying to understand the cyclical characteristics of the industry have to be the primary drivers.

Oil service companies are a classic example. Over long periods of time oil service companies will return the cost of capital and in down cycles their leverage will bankrupt them or come very close. They could be viewed as levered options on the energy complex and US economy. The point of Figure 8.1 is to demonstrate the volatility of commodity-driven capex-intensive companies. Since the inception of the

FIGURE 8.1   US Oil Services index 1997 to October 2019

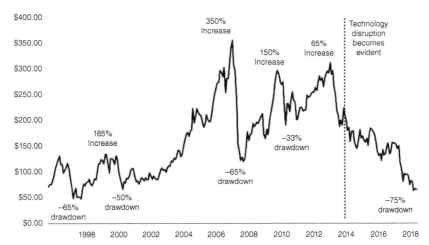

Oil Services index in 1997, there have been five drawdowns greater than 33% or one every four to five years. The breadth and depth of the drawdown is driven by the concept of *sunk costs* driving market prices for oil services to cash expense costs and below. If you own oil rigs in a down cycle period, you have already purchased the rigs and your capital is in the asset. You are most likely going to try and win contracts at prices that are well below the real cost of capital for the business. You are going to bid out your assets at whatever price level it takes to win and bring cash in the door to pay your debt service and the employees who have to be kept to run the business. Capex-intensive companies will drive prices below any reasonable return on capital levels in times of stress.

Of course, you also have incredible upside returns every four to five years as the cycle rebounds and assets have not been purchased during the trough period, which makes them scarce in a rebound and drives prices significantly higher. If you can time the bottom of a cycle in an industry like this, you can make a significantly superior return, but timing cycles is more difficult than it may appear. When we discuss portfolio management in chapter 11, we will also discuss the behavioral mistakes that are more likely when holding very volatile positions that are cycle driven.

The final and most serious problem with capex-intensive companies is disruption-driven paradigm shifts. We have already discussed at length the accelerated pace of disruption, which makes the future of investing in capex-intensive companies bleaker than the past. In the oil services chart in Figure 8.1, you can see that the 75% drawdown starting in 2013 was both cyclical and disruptive. Fracking technology and energy renewables growth was not a completely unknown concern going into 2013, but the investor sentiment turned from concern to the belief that there was a paradigm shift occurring, and oil rigs and well maintenance were never going to rebound to prior cyclical highs due to fracking-driven production increases and renewable-driven demand decreases. The final verdict is not out on this paradigm shift, but you can see the difficulty in making money in companies like this and the opportunity for large losses.

Roll-up acquisition strategy

Roll-ups are companies being managed with the explicit strategy to consolidate a fragmented industry. They are the extreme case of acquisition growth. Hedge fund managers are often attracted to roll-ups due to the potential growth. Various corporate executives have created reputations that excite investors based on their prior success in roll-up ventures. The pitch to investors is relatively simple: the company will buy smaller companies in a fragmented industry creating operating synergies on the cost side and the ability to offer customers both better service and better pricing due to the lower cost structure and enhanced operational capabilities of the larger company. As an extra bonus, the acquisitions will be done at valuation multiples below the company's public valuation multiple, creating financial engineering benefits that accrue to shareholders. Roll-up strategies are also a favorite of private equity investors, because they build platforms to acquire companies. Adding leverage to the equation only enhances the financial engineering benefits and volatility. This strategy is better in the private markets than the public markets, because quarterly earnings projections are difficult and public company disclosure hurts confidentiality.

A characteristic of roll-up strategies that should be acknowledged is that they always look great in a spreadsheet analysis, but are much harder to be successful in reality. Adding revenues each quarter from new acquisitions financed with debt, while simultaneously levering expenses, creates a very compelling financial projection spreadsheet. Unfortunately this completely ignores the operational problems and acquisition delays that are inherent to the strategy and are generally not illustrated in a spreadsheet.

After analyzing roll-up performance history, the results are very similar to overall individual company M&A success analyses that historically have demonstrated a probability of success to be between 30% and 50% using time periods of three to seven years—not a very compelling hit rate. Harvard, Wharton, McKinsey, and others have done work on the factors affecting success and many cite the number one reason for failure to be cultural fit and human capital problems in the integration. Not surprisingly, the difference with roll-up strategy success is that the range of outcomes is wider, because the company is more levered to acquisition risk.

There are a few key considerations in investing in roll-ups. The first is that management is more important than usual and their ability to articulate a defined process for target selection, valuation, and execution of integration into the parent company is the first hurdle to considering the investment. The articulation of the strategy is important, because management needs to sell Wall Street analysts and investors on their story to create a valuation multiple high enough to allow the use of their public stock as acquisition currency. When a roll-up company's valuation multiple is low and cost of capital is very high, the strategy cannot work.

We will discuss management teams later, but the problem with dependence on a management team is the difficulty in assessing people. It is relatively easy to assess whether management is honest, hard-working, and has experience, but knowing that a management team fits this specific undertaking at this point in their careers is difficult. It is also not just understanding the roll-up company management team but also the interactions with all the other management teams being purchased. Humans are hard to forecast. At their core, roll-ups are integrating people at a very fast pace.

If you can get past this management hurdle and consider making the investment, you must acknowledge that at some point in the next few years the stock will implode and be down 30% or more. Some roll-ups come back to set new highs, and the process cycles through again as new expectations are created, but every roll-up has at least one moment (if not many) of extreme investor angst that makes selling broad and brutal. Here are some important questions to ask yourself:

- Can you be ready for this volatility and is it worth the trouble?
- How do you plan on managing the position within the portfolio?

If you are invested in the roll-up company for fundamental business reasons and think the company is truly adding value to both customers and shareholders by consolidating the industry, it is important to recognize that many other shareholders are not invested for that reason. They are momentum investors that think it's a sexy story; if it gets rocky they are going to move onto the next hot stock. The volatility of both the stock and earnings are issues a manager needs to be prepared for when entering a roll-up investment.

Why do roll-ups implode at some point in the public markets?

The typical roll-up company begins in a fast and furious manner as the management team touts their strategy on Wall Street, which they do to both help their stock compensation plans and because they need their stock to be valued highly to allow for acquisitions to be done at reasonable prices. If the CEO has been involved with a successful roll-up in the past, the story is better. This creates excitement among investors, such as hedge funds, and the stock starts to move and attracts momentum investors. The company starts making acquisitions usually at a fast pace, which drives sales growth and makes for great early investor earnings calls as sales ramp higher. These great early earnings releases attract more momentum investors.

The roll-up company deal team finds acquisition targets, negotiates deals, and turns it over to the legal team to complete. The legal team finishes and hands it off to the operational integration team; meanwhile, the deal team is finished negotiating a new deal. The deals build on each other. If this were a purely technical process, maybe it would run smoothly, but acquisitions and integration involve people. As noted previously, the number one reason acquisitions fail is due to culture or people issues. The business owners and teams of the newly acquired companies do not always integrate smoothly into the parent company assembly line. In fact, almost by definition, business owners do not like the idea of being part of a larger company and they push back on changes and often quit. In a 20-year analysis of entrepreneurial activity by PriceWaterhouse, it was found that over 70% of entrepreneurs left their company within a year after it was sold. Company founders are often integral to success, but difficult to keep involved and incentivized after being acquired.

Company integrations are more often messy than smooth. That does not mean that they cannot get fixed after a few rocky months; it just means the strategy looks a lot cleaner and smoother on the analyst's spreadsheet than it can ever be in reality. On the spreadsheet, there are three acquisitions every quarter and 8% quarter over quarter growth with a 50 basis point margin increase every quarter. In reality a few large customers are lost, some owners quit, and unforeseen expenses crop up. Invariably the public roll-up management team glosses over these issues with their public shareholders using the rationalization that they are minor setbacks in the broader compelling opportunity.

At the same time as new acquisitions are being integrated, all the other business owners in the industry have become aware of the roll-up occurring, because it is big industry news. They get busy either preparing their business for stronger competition or putting some touch-up paint on their business in preparation for the call from the roll-up deal team. They prepare for a negotiation where they think they can ask for two to three times the value they ever dreamed of previously.

There always comes a point when the roll-up management team has to hold an earnings call when they say everything is not going as smoothly as expected and they have to slow the acquisition pace. The reason may be to give the integration team a chance to catch up, because deals are not as quickly completed as expected, or they have a few operational issues to work out. The company cuts forecasts and all the momentum investors exit causing a significant drop in the stock price. At this point everyone starts to question the original thesis and if a roll-up will work in this specific industry. All might not be lost; it might just be that operational reality is messy and does not fit quarterly earnings guidance. A good management team may be able to stabilize things and get back to buying companies in six months or a year; many go on to become successful. Regardless, there will be stress and volatility.

So roll-ups can be successful investments, but they will be volatile and pain is part of the process every time. Understanding the organic growth and margin potential is critical. Additionally, understanding the type of due diligence process needed (talking to business owners and customers continually), knowing how to look for signs of the stress coming, and managing the position appropriately in your portfolio is the way to succeed in roll-up investments.

Other types of companies to be wary of

Every year has a few stocks that lots of hedge funds are talking about and trading in. The stocks become very volatile as speculators take sides. Normal public investing is hard enough, because you have to watch stock movements every day that have no relationship to fundamental business change. If the price of a stock starts moving up and down 5% daily based on whispers of different short-term data points or a short sellers report, the investment may be too speculative. The volatility may overwhelm the fundamentals. These stocks are entertaining to talk about and watch, but often not to hold in a portfolio. One could take the approach that you are going to do better work and hold through the volatility, but wild volatility can cause behavioral mistakes in portfolio management. High volatility in one portfolio position can also affect other portfolio decisions due to the short-term effect on returns. It may not be worth the stress to be invested in the hotly traded stocks of the moment.

Highly levered companies may be an obvious group of companies to tread lightly in, but there is real benefit to equity holders in a company that manages their balance sheet efficiently. For this reason, simply avoiding all companies with leverage is too stringent. The financial engineering that occurs, especially in the low interest rate environment that we may be in for a long time, is a significant return driver. The focus should be on the combination of balance sheet leverage and volatility of operating margins. Although most investors analyze the current net debt/EBITDA (earnings before interest, tax, depreciation, and amortization) and interest coverage ratios, the most important analysis is stressing operating margins and sales in relation to the current debt load. Companies with very stable margins can handle debt, but cyclical companies often cannot handle the amount of debt they take on in good economic times.

There is a natural but dangerous business, credit, and capex-intensive company relationship, as illustrated in the following graphic. When economic demand is strong, cyclical companies want to produce more. In order to produce more, they need to increase capex. Because the economy is good, lenders are relaxing lending standards and making loans. Capex is spent, supply is increased to meet demand and sales, margins and debt loads increase. When the economy slows, sales drop, margins drop, lenders no longer want to lend or extend loans, and the equity holders bear the brunt of the high debt service and bankruptcy concerns. So the important analysis is not that the company net debt/EBITDA is 2.0 times today, but what it would be if EBITDA dropped back to the prior trough level. Performing this stressed EBITDA analysis will often make the opportunity look much less compelling. In the current environment, many highly levered companies have been able to tread water as low rates and an extended business cycle have kept them afloat.

Business, Capex, and Credit Cycle

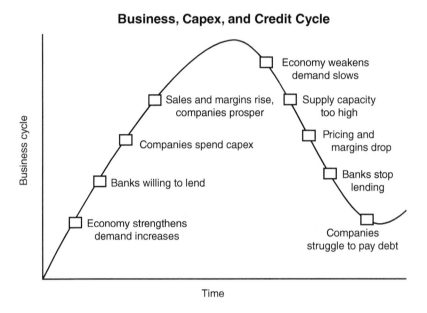

What to look for in a company: Sales growth

It may seem counterintuitive to have started with what you do not want to own, but it is actually easier to determine bad risk and reward opportunities than good ones. If you think through all the company types described so far, you will be able to either completely avoid or tread carefully in more than 30% of the broad US equity universe. This is both an alpha-producing and time-saving top-down process.

From the remaining 70% of the universe, finding those few companies that you believe can be long-term winners and create significant outperformance is difficult and time-consuming. Top down analysis on historic return on equity, operating margins, and sales growth can help to focus research work, but as the process becomes bottom up (company by company) the analysis becomes more time-consuming. Often good ideas come from many sources, such as prior work on different companies and industry conferences.

When trying to find a long-term outperforming company, there has to be some growth driver. It doesn't have to be an incredibly high-growth company, but if there is no avenue for at least high single-digit sustainable growth the company won't be able to sustain returns. When analyzing top quintile performance returns over the last 20 years, about 90% had average revenue growth over 5%. This may be somewhat obvious and does not help the ability to forecast growth, but it defines a clear point of process in the investment thesis.

- **First, specifically define the sustainable long-term growth driver of the business.**

Growth can come through a number of strategies. Some strategies are easier to forecast and some are more difficult to envision. In addition to understanding the company's strategy it is also important to think about the addressable market and whether there is new untapped market growth (called *whitespace*) or whether the industry is mature and each dollar of growth will have to be taken from some other player in the industry. Investing in industries with organic revenue tailwinds is simply easier than fighting a mature market. In the United States, many companies with sustainable growth strategies are disruptors in either a major industry transforming way or in taking market share from the established players. Either way, every dollar of growth has to be taken from a competitor. In many emerging markets, industries are still in their infancy and new consumers are entering the middle class. Revenues can increase without having to take every dollar from a competitor, because new market growth is occurring.

As an example in the restaurant industry, Shake Shack did not transform the industry, but it offered a product that captured consumer interest and demand and could take market share from established competitors. In this type of situation, the focus has to be on the product and whether it is truly a product that will move customers away from their normal routine. In Brazil, Burger King is expanding and growing as the number three fast food company in the country. It would be hard to tout Burger King as having a truly better product than their competitors, but in this case it is not needed. There is room for new growth in Brazil and they don't have to take share from the number one or two players. The middle class in Latin America is growing at about 8% per year and the Brazilian fast food industry only accounts for 10% of the out-of-home food industry compared to almost 50% in the United States. In the Burger King Brazil example, the emphasis needs to be on the overall market growth and operational roll-out strategy. Different types of growth are discussed, in order of ease of forecasting.

- **Unit growth.** Unit growth is the easiest to forecast. A unit-driven business model can exist in a wide variety of industries: obviously retail stores and restaurants, but also tax centers, propane distribution, fitness centers, and pest control businesses. The key is a business where a few units can be designed, tested, and perfected in one geography and then expanded to other geographies. Once the executives and investors have an understanding of the capex needed and four wall contribution of an individual unit, the growth is relatively easy to forecast. Unit growth businesses with a strong return on invested capital in emerging markets where there is population and income growth can be one of the most compelling investment opportunities today.

- **Product and sku (stockkeeping unit) growth.** Growth opportunities where a brand or product has been created and gained some customer traction and is now trying to grow that brand through new distribution channels and/or sku growth are probably the second easiest to forecast. Obviously, the product, brand, and customer acceptance have to be the focus. The other big issue that can often be problematic in this type of growth opportunity is the distribution channel dynamics. Who has the strength in negotiating power? Is it the distribution channel partner or the product suppliers? If product suppliers have the power they can drive both growth and margins in this type of expansion. If distribution channel partners have power, they will always take a significant portion of the margin as the product company grows.

  In some cases, the growth is driven by internal sales team expansion. That may be the best strategy, but investors have to be ready for a stair-step type of growth, as opposed to linear growth. Expanding sales teams will incur expenses and hurt margins before they gain new customer traction and create new sales. In the public markets two quarters of operating expense growth without matching sales growth can cause a negative stock reaction. For fundamental investors with longer time horizons, this could create buying opportunities. As long as fundamental investors understand what is happening, they can have conviction to buy on these opportunities and manage their portfolio position well.

- **Vertical industry growth.** Businesses that have performed very well in one industry and are now expanding to other industries are significantly tougher to forecast, because industries have very specific needs, switching costs, and sales cycles. A company like Salesforce.com has done an incredible job in creating a great product but also being able to transform the product to be a market leader in each industry vertical they enter. There are many other software companies that can provide a great product to one industry but are not going to be able to expand outside that industry. Specific industry expertise is not always easily gained, and expanding product offerings across industry verticals is often harder than first imagined.

- **Best in class technology/R&D/human talent.** Businesses that provide a product or service that need a continual stream of new ideas or new people to grow can be difficult to forecast, because the sustainability is unclear. The debate is often over whether the innovation or best-in-class product is due to specific people or whether it has been ingrained into the culture. Apple might be a good example, where they have had an incredible history of innovation for almost two decades. However, if you are buying the company today and need to define a specific growth driver for the 2020s, what is it? Can you count on the Apple culture to spur innovation or was it Steve Jobs? Companies that may be perceived as creating a culture that spans decades might be Goldman Sachs or Accenture. They historically have recruited the best talent for years and their brand and success create a virtuous cycle of attracting talent and continuing their leadership position in the industry. Understanding if a company has built a sustainable culture of innovation and attracting superior human talent is difficult.

• **Low-cost advantage growth.** Businesses that can provide a low-cost advantage to their clients in a long-term sustainable manner are becoming fewer and fewer, because supply chains are easy to replicate and competition is high. If a market is large and capital is plentiful, competition will enter to meet low-cost providers by accepting a lower operating margin. This can cause intense industry competition and a race to the bottom from a margin perspective. Everyone loves to pay less for a product, but the difficulty in forecasting is to understand why the low-cost advantage is sustainable and not just a short-term advantage. TJ Maxx, the discount fashion retailer, would be one example of a business that has been able to sustain a low-cost advantage in their retail niche. They do so through brand relationships that allow them access to products that are both unique and cheaper than their smaller competitors.

> *Look for companies with niches.*
>
> —*Peter Lynch*

Low-cost advantage can occur in the commodity complex due to best-in-class assets, but in the commodity complex it is hard to envision sustainable long-term growth due to the cyclicality. The best example of success in this area would be Martin Marietta, but even their asset and location-driven cost advantage is subject to both real cyclicality and market-expected cyclicality. Real cyclicality hits sales growth and expected cyclicality is evidenced by severe periods of market multiple compression. Unfortunately, market multiple compression can create large losers, even if fundamentals remain strong.

• **A new future.** The toughest company to forecast is the company that is pioneering an entirely new market or often a product for a market that people expect to exist in five or ten years. This is where venture capitalists earn their fees. In the public markets paying high multiples for future growth in a market that does not really exist today is something to avoid. Few public investors are successful in this area. To be clear, the top quintile of venture capital firms have been very successful, but once these companies hit the public markets high expectations are priced into the valuation. The combination of high expectations, high valuation, and high volatility of future cash flows is not the right combination for sustainable success.

Those are the primary types of growth drivers to be understood and forecasted in defining the investment thesis. Considering whether the company can execute on one or often a combination of the growth drivers is the first area of focus. Assuming a company can pass the sales growth hurdle, the second focus is operating margins.

What to look for in a company: Operating margins

- Will operating margins improve with sales?
- Where is the business model leverage?
- How sustainable is the margin improvement?

There are often quite a few opportunities in the public markets, where a company has a very compelling plan to increase operating margins through operational efficiencies of one kind or another, but they don't have an avenue for growth. As an example, a US home furnishings company may have a strong traditional brand name and have produced 8% operating margins for the last decade, but now they have a plan to sell the factory they own for cash (sale-leaseback), streamline personnel, and add state-of-the-art supply chain technology. The company expects to increase margins from 8% to 14% in three to five years. This is an opportunity where you will make money, if you are correct. You may achieve a 50% to 100% return over three years, which is a good investment, but not the five-plus-year 25% compounding portfolio leader that we have been discussing. One drawback to this type of investment is the reinvestment risk. If the company achieves its plan and the investment is successful, you must sell and find another opportunity just as compelling. There is no chance the margin turnaround story will produce strong returns for many years.

One of the most important elements of security selection and portfolio management is understanding what type of investment you are making. Is it a long-term compounding opportunity, intermediate-term margin recovery opportunity, or a very-high-risk option opportunity? As we will discuss in portfolio management (chapter 11), classifying investments by time horizon and risk will help greatly in determining how to manage the investment in the portfolio as the stock price moves.

Growing top line sales should naturally increase the operating margin, but hopefully there is operational leverage in the business model and margins can increase at a faster rate than sales. The two most important elements in operating margin improvement are gross margin and marketing expenses. General and administrative (G&A) expenses are a smaller part of the cost structure and will naturally be levered as sales increase at a predictable pace. Research and development (R&D) could be easily leveraged but is often maintained at a variable percent of sales to maintain innovation. We will dig into the major issues affecting gross margin and the sales-to-marketing expense relationship.

Gross margin can be increased (affected) in three major ways:

- **Economies of scale.** Economies of scale in the buying process will lower costs. Gross margin expense savings may be on the actual commodity cost purchase or finished product purchases. As an example, Nike buys finished product of one million shoes in an individual purchase order when they bought 500,000 shoes in the past. Compared to Goodyear who buys rubber in bulk quantities for tires. They are both economies of scale but different in execution. The pure commodity exposure is more volatile and less predictable. Companies with cost structures that have a heavy reliance on commodity prices should be viewed more negatively due to the price volatility. The obvious question that parallels this concern is whether the company has a strong enough position to pass on extraordinary commodity increases to its customers. From a research perspective, understanding the availability of substitutes and the importance of your product to the customer is a focus. If a product does not have a substitute and purchases cannot be put off for long periods of time by the customer, an extraordinary commodity cost expense can usually be passed on to the customer, because all competing companies are facing the same extra cost. Commodities may have a benign effect in this scenario. If there is a viable substitute for the product, then it is a major problem and is most likely a reason to pass on investing. Inability to pass on a commodity cost increase to the customer would demonstrate that the product itself is commodity-like, which is a structural issue in any business model trying to provide high returns on equity.

Distribution economies of scale would also fall under this category. Distribution economies of scale are driven by the ability to bring in or ship out product in a cheaper way through scale. Understanding how the business cost structure and supply chain works will enable an understanding of the potential impact.

- **Process improvements.** Gross margin expenses can also be cut as the management team becomes more sophisticated over time and can add value in the engineering or product development process. It will not be a linear savings, but sophistication of the product development process should be an additive factor over time. This is also an interesting metric to keep track of in relation to forming an opinion on the strength of the management team.
- **Technology advancements.** Technology from outside the industry can be used to cut costs. Whether it be the use of robotics or artificial intelligence, the general advancement of technology can increase efficiency. As was discussed in a previous chapter, technological advancements will have a strong impact on company efficiencies in the 2020s as more and more data can be analyzed. Understanding the magnitude and potential of technology changes is now central to understanding every industry.

Sales and marketing expenses in relation to sales growth is probably the most important metric to monitor in a long-term investment. If a company product or service is being embraced by customers, you will see the evidence in this metric. A compelling product creates word-of-mouth referrals, which is the most productive way to sell. Companies that have high customer satisfaction will almost always lever their marketing expenses. Digging into the relationship between sales and various marketing expenses will shed light on what type of marketing works best and create a better understanding of the specific market. For this reason, this metric should be detailed in as many ways as possible. Customer acquisition cost, average order size per customer, and customer churn are a few metrics in this category. There is no one metric that is more important than all others, but a company leveraging sales and marketing expense is a great indicator of success.

What to look for in a company: Market power sustainability

In analyzing the potential for sales and operating margin growth, there are areas that should be focused on to indicate whether this growth is sustainable. Looking at a business through these various lenses will separate short-term, periodic success from long-term sales and earnings growth success.

Although it was written in 1979, Michael Porter's *Competitive Strategy* structure is still a great place to start in analyzing the long-term sustainability of a company. Focusing only on a company's direct peer competition is a mistake. Competition is more complex than peer-to-peer competition, and Porter's model of five forces takes that into account.

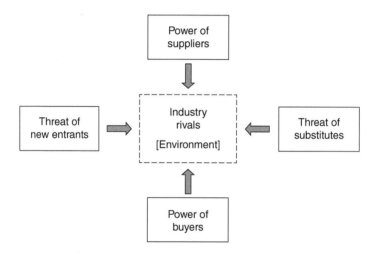

In today's accelerated pace of technology environment, where disruption is occurring at record rates the threat of new entrants and threat of substitutes are more important than ever before. The entrance of technology firms into almost every industry will only continue in the 2020s. Their involvement in the competitive environment may be as a new entrant or creator of a substitute product. No company is going to look perfect in a Porter five forces analysis or it would be a monopoly, but understanding the issues you should be monitoring before they become apparent to the rest of the market is an information research advantage.

- **Pricing power.** Pricing power is a great indicator of a company's long-term growth sustainability. The obvious point is that customers will pay more for a product only when they are happy with the value proposition. There are subtler additional points, though. Increasing pricing is possible only when your customers are healthy and healthy customers are important to any business. If you are selling into an industry under stress, customers may love your product but may be forced to look for a cheaper alternative due to their financial situation. It is also important to understand your customer's cost structure and how essential your product is to their business. A great scenario is when your product is essential to the buyer but not a very large part of their cost structure. Being a small part of their cost structure enables you to increase prices 10% without putting the customer under stress. If their product costs $10 to produce and you sell them a $1.00 part, a 10 cent increase will not be that painful. If you are selling a customer an $8 part in their $10 cost structure, a 10% increase will be harder to pass through.

- **Switching costs.** Switching costs are the costs incurred by consumers or businesses as a result of their changing products. The cost can be monetary, but it is often a result of the time it takes to learn new activities and change company processes. Switching costs parallels pricing power in some ways, because high switching costs usually allow pricing power. Switching costs can be driven by educational hurdles, initial starting expenses, and operational dependence. High switching costs add value to any business model, but they need to be monitored for changes in the competitive environment, because new technologies may be able to lower switching costs at some point in the future.

> *Buy companies with strong histories of profitability and with a dominant business franchise.*
>
> —*Warren Buffett, investor*

- **Intangibles.** Intangible assets, including brands, patents, and licenses, are always a focus in company analysis. Analyzing brand strength can be done through focus groups and surveys. It can also be done by analyzing pricing strategies across the industry and determining who can charge more or less for their product. Pricing strategies may be associated with product-specific issues but can also be tied back to brand strength. Patents and licenses obviously add to sustainability, but the history of regulation in the company's geography should be understood. Licenses are only as good as government regulation allows them to be and patents are only enforced in countries with strong rules of law and for a limited time period.

- **Network effect.** Network effect is the positive effect of each new user adding value to the current product, which creates a virtuous cycle of growth and market share gain. In public investing, network effect–oriented companies usually have already reached a heathy critical mass of users and are in the midst of experiencing benefits from the network effect. In venture capital investing, companies are in their infancy and the network effect can be hoped for, but often cannot yet be seen, because the tipping point of critical mass has not been achieved. A network effect is very hard to create, but once achieved it is very powerful. Network effects in combination with brand and pricing power are particularly powerful.

The threat of new entrants and substitution should be closely analyzed in relation to the network effect. If a company is demonstrating strong network effects it is most likely leading its current direct competitors and direct threats are not high.

New entrant or substitute products are often the challengers to monitor. LinkedIn, a business professionals networking site, has experienced a very strong network effect as it has grown. Each new person added to the network creates more value for those already on the network. LinkedIn does not have a significant direct competitive threat, because they won the market share war in years past. However the new entrance of Google, Apple, or Facebook, who already have very large user networks, would be a serious threat. Since LinkedIn users are already in those ecosystems, switching costs would be lower, and LinkedIn's network competitive value would be diminished.

- **Distribution.** Distribution can be a valuable asset. If a company has a faster, better, cheaper way to get a product to the end user, it can be a strong competitive advantage. Pure distribution companies are usually low margin businesses, but there are some companies that are vertically integrated. They provide the product and have a unique distribution system that they control. Being vertically integrated can often be a powerful competitive position. As an example, Essilor Luxottica, a European eyewear company, designs, manufactures, and distributes sunglasses through thousands of stores and kiosks around the world. They own the distribution channel that a competitor would want to access to sell their product. To maintain satisfied end customers, they may offer products other than their own in their retail stores, but their power allows them to set terms and sustain a dominant positioning. Vertically controlling an industry is a very powerful, long-term advantage.

In the descriptive analysis of competitive factors, I have not used the term *barriers to entry*, which is common terminology in discussing investment and business strategy. Many of the issues addressed are, in fact, barriers to entry, but I believe *growth sustainability* is a better way to think about the analysis. The reason is, from an investing perspective, you would prefer a company whose barriers to entry are protecting growth. There are companies that have barriers to entry but are not growing. The barriers are helpful in maintaining the status quo, but the industry is mature or declining. As an example, the distribution channel, production economies of scale, and global strength of the Coca-Cola brand are clearly strong barriers to entry, but soda consumption is on the decline and the company has not grown in a decade. The strong barriers to entry are not sustaining growth, they are protecting from sales declines. Having a growth driver was the first hurdle in our search, and the goal is to find companies who have barriers to avoid the competitive environment from changing the forecasted growth, hence *growth sustainability*.

Management teams

Management is key to any successful business. It is also the most difficult element to assess. You are not only assessing the individuals managing the business but also you need to assess what their contribution will be and how important a factor they will be in the future success or failure. From meeting with hundreds of companies from start-ups to global market leaders, my experience is that an investment security selection focus on management becomes less important as the company becomes larger.

Conceptually, in Figure 8.2, start-ups and micro-cap companies have a higher need for good management to become successful. As you analyze larger and larger companies, the effect management has on outcomes gets smaller and smaller. It is still important, but less so. The variance of management talent follows the same pattern. It is very high in small companies, where you can have great management teams and you can have very weak management teams.

The core management team in very small companies is not surrounded by a dozen other MBAs and backed by an experienced board. The variance in management talent across large cap public companies is not that wide. To become the CEO of a large public company you must be experienced and successful, because you were chosen over many educated and driven candidates. From a security selection analysis standpoint, 10% of large cap management teams are exceptional, potentially visionaries. Another 10% are destroying value and should be avoided by investors. The other 80% are solid, experienced management teams that are quite hard to rank among each other. Picking the 10% of management teams that are visionaries is easy in hindsight and very difficult in real time. When investing in large cap companies, time should be spent to make sure you are not in one of the bottom 10% of value-destroying management teams. Beyond that, it may not be possible to add a lot more value. Rarely are investment managers very successful in adding security selection value by a detailed

FIGURE 8.2   Management and company size

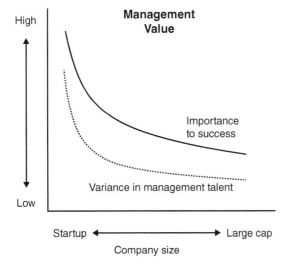

ranking of a the many solid management teams. When investing in illiquid private or public micro-cap companies, management talent should be top priority and an early hurdle that must be crossed or there is no reason to invest.

One other parallel factor to management teams is company culture. Company culture can be easier to assess than management, because it is pervasive across the company's employees. A particularly strong or innovative company culture can drive success and should be considered in the investment thesis. The importance of culture in security selection often mirrors the importance of management. In mid and large cap companies there are a few instances of very positive, innovative cultures that make a difference to the business; then there are a few very bad cultures that should be avoided. The majority of company cultures are generally positive but are not a determining factor in stock performance. Like management teams company culture is more of a determining factor in young, fast-growing companies.

Being contrarian and time horizon

Many successful investors will cite taking a contrarian approach as one of the most important elements in security selection and in overall performance. This makes sense, because in-line market thinking will create in-line results. However, many hear "be contrarian" to mean buy cheap stocks. Being contrarian can be just as effective in buying long-term compounding companies, if they are bought at times of overall market stress or short-term setbacks associated with the company. Knowing your long-term compounding company well enough to be contrarian and add exposure when the market is scared is the best way of being contrarian.

> *The best thing that happens to us is when a great company gets into temporary trouble. We want to buy them when they're on the operating table.*
> —*Warren Buffett, investor*

A successful contrarian has a comprehensive group of attractive companies that are monitored regularly. When you get a contrarian opportunity to invest, you will be ready. In this scenario, being a contrarian mirrors patience and valuation. Buy and sell targets will be discussed in detail in the next chapter. They can provide a road map for entering companies you like at disciplined, contrarian entry points. This process becomes part of good portfolio management.

Security selection and the ability to be contrarian must be considered in the context of a time horizon. On entering an investment, the investment thesis should have a concept of the time horizon for the investment position to reach its potential. It may be long term, in which case you hope to monitor continually and continue to raise your buy and sell targets ever higher and push the time horizon out farther. Other investments may have much more stringent time horizons, because they do not have the growth sustainability necessary to be a long-term investment.

The biggest mistake in investing is believing the last three years is representative of what the next three years is going to be like.

—*Ray Dalio, investor*

It's worth repeating that time horizon is a great asset to an investment manager and that the only way this advantage can be attained is to have the manager and capital allocator aligned in their time horizon expectations. With all the challenges to time horizon we have discussed, managers need to recognize its importance and proactively approach the problem in three ways.

The first is to try and raise capital from sophisticated and patient investors who can offer this advantage to their managers and share in its rewards. This is a great solution, but not always controllable, and there are always changes in the needs of capital allocators and demands that are unforeseeable.

The second way is to be very specific in defining unique time horizons for different issues and catalysts in each investment thesis. Expecting the company to achieve growth in cash flows in three years may be a general time horizon expectation, but it is better to be specific in each section of the investment thesis. Over what time period is a certain product expected to come to market? Over what time period are customer acquisition costs expected to improve? Having unique time horizon expectations for different issues will help make a decision to hold or cut the investment position easier as time passes. Having a specific time line and milestones in mind for the company's progress adds value to the research process.

The third way is to simply recognize the importance of time horizon pressure on behavioral portfolio management decisions. Consciously understanding the pressure to sell winners to demonstrate completed positive investment decisions or to sell declining investments too early to lower volatility will help avoid some of the behavioral mistakes we will discuss in the portfolio management chapter (chapter 11).

When is having conviction and being contrarian being blind to an investment mistake?

Of course, there is no one answer. This has always been one of the most important decisions for a successful investment manager. No manager likes losses, but thinking back to some of the original data we looked at pertaining to excess returns by decile, one key was to avoid investing in any of the ninth and tenth decile–returning companies. Poor performers can destroy all the profits from your other winning positions. All the challenges driven by low rates and disruption discussed in Part I are pressuring this decision more than it has been historical.

A few ideas to consider.

First the more specific the investment thesis was written and documented throughout the investment period, the better prepared you will be to make the decision: better process, better decisions.

Second, focusing on balance sheet issues is a key at this decision point. When initiating the investment, the focus was most likely on the income and cash flow statements, but now downside scenarios need to be the focus. Companies with balance sheet leverage are very problematic in the decision to hold on to a struggling invest-ment, because the downside is a total loss of equity capital. The business may have a strong brand or product that will maintain some value even in dire periods, but in a levered company that does not mean that the current equity investors will be around to participate in a future recovery. So balance sheet leverage is a real reason to give up and move on from an investment.

Third, if the growth drivers or industry have significantly changed from the orig-inal thesis, the investment should be sold. Where investment managers often fail is when they change the investment thesis without fully acknowledging that change. A long-term growth investment thesis may be changed after two years of company problems to be a margin recovery thesis or a cheap valuation thesis. A change in investment thesis type (*thesis creep*) is a strong indicator of holding too long.

CHAPTER 9

VALUATION

- *Importance of valuation in fundamental versus value investing*
- *Fundamental investing: Big picture*
- *Owner's yield*
- *Free cash flow as an important metric*
- *Company balance sheet leverage*
- *Price target creation and channels*

After finding good businesses, success depends on buying them at a price that makes economic sense and allows for outperformance. This chapter will describe a valuation process to complement security selection. The two pieces have to go hand in hand to be successful.

Company earnings, cash flow creation, and capital allocation will be accurately reflected in stock prices, fortunately not on a weekly, monthly, or even quarterly basis but almost always within a three-year period. This short-term price dislocation paradigm is a big part of what enables experienced fundamental investors to create superior returns. These valuation dislocations happen for a host of reasons: the market's inability to understand a company's growth potential, the market's concern over industry changes, the market's focus on macro concerns, and many other non-company cash flow specific reasons.

The Bank of America Merrill Lynch quantitative strategy analysis of the predictive power of valuation in Figure 9.1 illustrates the long-term importance of valuation in making investment decisions. In holding an investment for eight years, valuation is shown to be 50% of the contributing factor to returns. It also demonstrates how long the public markets can make valuation a nonfactor. In the first two years, valuation is less than 20% of the contributing factor to returns. The market goes through regimes, where high valuations will be supported for long periods of time or certain sectors will be strongly in and out of favor for periods of time.

Again, reflecting on time horizon, if you are a manager who is trying to create returns in a one-year period to impress clients, valuation should not be a large part of your decision process. Momentum is a more predictive factor in a one-year return analysis. If you jump from momentum stock to momentum stock, you may have a

FIGURE 9.1   Predictive power of valuation over time 1987 to June 2019

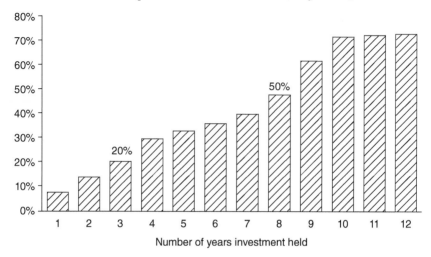

Number of years investment held

few good years in a row, but then there will be a very poor period wiping out the prior returns. Investing in a repeatable, sustainable process must take valuation into account to produce outperformance through cycles. The effect of investment managers losing assets to passive investing alternatives is that they become focused on monthly returns to stem the outflows of capital. This leads to an inability to be patient, contrarian, and a true fundamental investor. It leads to more investors following the herd into momentum stocks. This cycle will offer additional opportunities for the remaining long-term investors, because they take advantage of others making short-term decisions. However, momentum can rule the markets for a long time, and it pushes the definition of long term out from three to five years. It demands more patience from fundamental investors and their clients.

> *Do not take yearly results too seriously. Instead, focus on four- or five-year averages.*
>
> —*Warren Buffett, investor*

Importance of valuation in fundamental versus value investing

Fundamental investing is not the same as value investing. Value investing focuses on investing with a wide *margin of safety* (the difference between current stock price and the investor's fair value) as the way to achieve superior returns. Importantly, future forecasts are seen as too unpredictable to rely on, so a very heavy emphasis is put on current valuation metrics. The heavy emphasis on current valuation metrics means value investors buy cheap stocks. Stocks are usually cheap, when they are industry laggards, in out-of-favor industries or awaiting a cyclical recovery. Historically, industries do come back into favor and cycles reverse. Although this will, of course, still happen, it will not happen as often in an era of continual business disruption. Industries are being disrupted at a faster pace, which means value investors are more likely to be invested in a company that will never return to its former market positon. The earnings of these cheap companies will not mean revert, as frequently as they have in the past.

The concept of mean reversion is critical to the success of value investing. A paradigm shift is the antithesis of mean reversion and disruption creates paradigm shifts. As we have discussed, historic rates of mean reversion are being challenged by the confluence of central bank intervention and technological disruption. This has been the driver for value investing underperformance during the 2010s and it will continue in the 2020s.

This is not to say valuation does not matter. Valuation matters a lot, but you must understand future cash flows and their potential deterioration or expansion to be successful. Fundamental investing applies value investing concepts to the pursuit of superior business models and sustainable growth. These concepts may often be aligned with quality or growth investing methodologies, but there are subtle differences.

> *Buying a company with mediocre prospects just because the stock is cheap is a losing technique.*
>
> —*Peter Lynch, investor*

Fundamental investing: Big picture

A simple, big picture framework for fundamental investing is defined in the graphic. This is relatively intuitive, but we will dig into the nuances shortly. It is worth noting that the structure goes from left to right in order of easiest to analyze (current market valuation) to hardest to analyze (future forecast). Because simply selecting a company based on a cheap current day valuation may not add as much value in the future, managers have to work on the harder forecasting stage and be able to add value there. It should be acknowledged that the more the final target price is based on future cash flow forecasts, the greater chance an investor has to be wrong. This means putting the pieces together on a company with no current cash flows and a market valuation created solely by the expectation of future cash flows will be the most difficult analysis and the most prone to loss.

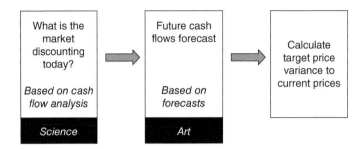

Fundamental investing is part science and part art. The *science* part is the analysis of what the current company is worth based on today's cash flows and the *art* part is in forecasting the future.

> *Much of the world is unknown and unpredictable. Thus, forecasting will always be an art.*
>
> —*Marty Whitman, investor*

Owner's yield

Understanding a company's valuation and specifically what the market is discounting in the future is the first step. There are many methodologies of valuing a company and all of them should be considered and reviewed for each investment. The benefit to looking at a company using different valuation metrics is it provides a deeper understanding of the company and can highlight different issues to be researched.

If a company looks cheap on an EV/EBITDA perspective, but not from a cash flow perspective, what is the issue hindering the company's cash flow generation? If it only looks cheap from a P/E perspective, is there something unique about the tax structure? Additionally, different valuations are better for some sectors and countries than others due to accounting issues. The single most compelling valuation methodology I have seen is *owner's yield*.

$$\text{Owners Yield} = \frac{\text{Cash Flow from Ops} - \text{Maintenance capex} + \text{Growth related expenses}}{\text{Market cap}}$$

Owner's yield emphasizes cash flow. Cash flow cuts through any accounting issues that may distort the valuation picture. Owner's yield separates cash outlays that are needed to maintain the current stream of cash flow and cash outlays that are growth related and are expected by management to increase cash flows in the future. This is the cleanest methodology to value what an investor receives by buying a share of stock. You are receiving cash flows from your current asset and you are using those cash flows to enhance your asset in some way to create better cash flows in the future. To make the best investment decision you need to understand both what the company has built to date and what it is building for the future.

The methodology is calculated in the form of yield (owner's cash flow divided by market cap), so it can be easily compared to the current yield curve and **equity risk premium.** Generally, the equity risk premium is calculated as the spread between the earnings yield (EPS/price) and the risk-free rate. This owner's yield methodology calculates the owner's yield spread to the ten-year Treasury rate. The idea behind this analysis is to think about whether you are being compensated adequately for the risk being taken relative to other investment opportunities.

In the current environment this creates a problem, because as we have discussed the developed world central banks are distorting their sovereign yield curves in a race to the bottom from a rate perspective. To address this issue, we will use the methodology based on today's yield curve, but we also compare it to an average historical yield curve. Reviewing both can help us further understand the valuation and how dependent the valuation is purely on the current yield curve distortion.

Free cash flow as an important metric

Free cash flow (cash flow from operations minus capex) is often discussed as an essential valuation metric. It is the capital available to be returned to shareholders, so in certain types of investment theses it may be a primary focus. The one problem with a strong free cash flow yield security selection emphasis is that it handicaps compelling growth companies unnecessarily. A company with low free cash flow may be very compelling if the reason for the low free cash flow is a large capital expenditure budget that is being spent well on high-return projects. A company with high free cash flow is good, but a company with high cash flow from operations being spent on new high return on equity projects is better.

In situations when you are investing in a company, sector, or geographical area because you believe in the future growth using free cash flow yield as a primary security selection metric can actually be negative to performance. If investing in Brazil is in large part based on an emerging market growth thesis, why would free cash flow be a primary security selection focus? You would like your Brazilian company to be taking advantage of the growth potential and putting capital back into high return on equity projects. *The security selection emphasis should be on growth, cash flow from operations, and the return on equity of new projects.*

Company balance sheet leverage

Balance sheet leverage is the other fundamental metric that is important to acknowledge in using owner's yield. You can't be fooled by a great owner's yield, because there is massive debt on the company balance sheet and the enterprise value dwarfs the market cap. To avoid this issue, we could use *owner's cash flow/enterprise value*. However that unnecessarily hurts companies that manage their capital structure efficiently, and debt can be productive for equity shareholders through financial engineering. The optimal amount of debt is an industry- and company-specific question, the key factors in the decision are volatility of the profit margins and cyclicality of sales. A company with historically stable margins that uses net debt levels of two times EBITDA in their capital structure should not be negatively viewed. An energy company with five times net debt to EBITDA and an extremely high variance in operating margins is just a commodity option, not a fundamental investment. Creating frameworks for levels of debt that are manageable for different industries is an important part of the valuation process to be used in conjunction with owner's yield. As we did in the top-down security selection process discussed in chapter 8, we can first remove companies with high risk debt profiles from the selection universe.

Price target creation and channels

To continue with the science part of the valuation analysis and creating company-specific price targets, an owner's cash flow can be projected and discounted back in the same way a traditional DCF analysis is done.

I have used Nike as an example in this section. Although you may have a different opinion, for this analysis we are assuming Nike is a premier global brand with best-in-class operational management. At a compelling valuation, it would be a stock that we would want to own and we would consider a *long-term compounder*. In Figure 9.2, the three-year return on equity for Nike demonstrates the high operational returns that the company has been able to achieve historically.

FIGURE 9.2 Nike three-year return on equity 2010 to October 2019

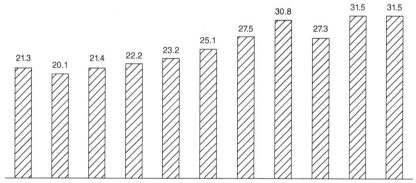

Source: Adapted from historic Nike public financial disclosures (10-Ks and 10-Qs).

FIGURE 9.3   Nike owner's cash flow yield analysis

Nike Stock Price $88.00								
Future period	1	2	3	4	5	6	7	
CFO growth rate		8%	3.0%	3.0%	3.0%	3.0%	3.0%	
Cash flow-ops	5,900	6,347	6,538	6,734	6,936	7,144	7,358	**Terminal**
Capex spend	(1,337)	(1,390)	(1,432)	(1,475)	(1,519)	(1,565)	(1,612)	**multiple**
% maint capex	50%	50%	50%	50%	50%	50%	50%	**12.00x**
R&D add back	0	0	0	0	0	0	0	**Terminal**
Owner's cash flow	5,232	5,652	5,822	5,996	6,176	6,362	6,552	**value**
EBITDA	6,218	7,104	7,317	7,536	7,762	7,995	8,235	**98,820**
Present value calculation	1	2	3	4	5	6	7	Terminal
PV discount factor	0.93	0.87	0.81	0.76	0.70	0.66	0.61	0.61
PV of owner's cash flows	4,477	4,914	4,719	4,532	4,353	4,180	4,014	60,543
PV value total	$91,732							
Shares outstanding	1,618.4							
Fair value stock price	**$56.68**							
Variance to current	*(36%)*							

The example in Figure 9.3 is a simple exercise in discounting back cash flow expectations, but no more complexity is necessary. Often we add complexity to a quantitative model to create an illusion of control, when being very exact about certain elements in a quantitative analysis that includes long-term forecasts that are volatile is not productive.

Owner's Cash Flow = Cash from Operations − Maintenance Capex

+ Growth related expenses

When we analyze the owner's cash flows of Nike, we have determined that 50% of the overall capex is used for maintenance capex, such as updating current stores, offices, and technology. The other 50% is growth capex. In considering the potential add back of growth-related expenses that were running through the income statement, we decided that their R&D and marketing expenses were necessary to maintain the current product offering pace. These were truly expenses and not producing future growth. The terminal value is created using an EBITDA multiple, which is an immediate indication that the model could not be wildly precise. The EBITDA multiple in a sale of Nike seven years in the future cannot be known and could range from as little as eight times to as high as 20+ times EBITDA. The cash flow forecasts are also highly dependent on future sales and margin results that will have a wide range of outcomes. We will take this range of outcomes into consideration by the creation of a buy and sell target channel, as opposed to creating a *fair value* single price target.

In a typical discounted cash flow analysis, a weighted average cost of capital (WACC) may be used for the discount rate. We have chosen to use an *investment hurdle rate,* which is based on the ten-year Treasury (for US companies) plus the equity risk premium multiplied by the company's beta. The reason is to ensure that we achieve a rate of return that exceeds what historical equities have achieved. In this situation, Nike's WACC is not very different than the investment hurdle used, but the idea is that we are comparing Nike to the average equity return, which we hope to outperform.

Investment hurdle = Risk − free rate + Equity risk premium × company beta

$$7.25\% = 3.00\% + 5.00\% \times 0.85$$

We have to recognize the effect central bank intervention has had on the equity markets in this type of analysis. The long-run historic equity risk premium is about 500 basis points, but it does vary widely and recently has been high affected by the drop in the US Treasury yield. For the Nike analysis, we used what we consider to be a more realistic long-term ten-year Treasury yield of 3.0%. As Treasury yields drop, discount rates drop and push up valuations in any discounted cash flow analysis. Using 3.0% as the ten-year Treasury resulted in a price of $57, when the ten-year Treasury yield was dropped 100bps to 2.0%, the target price increased to almost $65. This lower rate allows investors to feel they can pay more for companies, even though there is no change in future cash flows. In fact, risk to the future cash flows may be increasing. If the central banks are aggressively intervening in the markets to lower rates, they are probably quite concerned about the future economy. Is that a reason to increase your price target on a consumer discretionary company? Yet as risk-free rates have dropped throughout the 2010s, valuations have increased. Central banks count on investors to input the lower rates into their valuation models and decide to pay more for assets.

In Figure 9.4 the equity risk premium and ten-year Treasury yield are shown, which demonstrates the volatility of the equity risk premium and the move in the ten-year Treasury yield from 5% to 6% in the last 20 years to 2.0% today. The equity risk premium is wider today than historically by 200 basis points, which quantitatively makes equities more compelling and pushes investors into risk assets (equities), *the goal of the central bank*. We should remember the equity risk premium is high only because the ten-year Treasury yield is so low, not because Nike is cheap from an absolute perspective.

In the price target channel methodology, we recognize both our potential for error and the volatility of the equity risk premium, which is the same as the volatility of all other multiples (price to sales, price to earnings, and EV/EBITDA). In fact in a large cap company with stable margins, such as Nike, our potential error in cash flow forecasting is probably less than the potential fluctuation in multiples. The market gyrations around macro events are volatile and we do not want to buy or sell at the wrong time based on indiscriminate moves in the market affecting valuation multiples. After performing due diligence on Nike and determining it to be a long-term compounder, we would like to stay invested in the company unless we are proven

FIGURE 9.4   Equity risk premium and ten-year Treasury 2000 to October 2019

wrong about the company's fundamental operating results. We take on reinvestment risk and the risk of missing out on a great long-term investment return if we are continually selling stock at exactly the fair value created by a discounted owners cash flow analysis. The concept of fair value is not an exact science.

> *Prices fluctuate more than values—so therein lies opportunity.*
>
> —*Joel Greenblatt*

To illustrate the volatility in multiples and in recognition that this is not an exact science, we create channels that represent the potential fluctuations that we would consider common. From an equity risk premium perspective we might choose to hold the stock if it was only providing a 350 basis point premium and feel really great about it if we were receiving a 650 basis point equity premium. Because many people use EV/EBITDA multiples, this same methodology might translate to a fair value at 12 times EV/EBITDA with channels set at nine times EV/EBITDA on the low side and 15 times EV/EBITDA on the high side. Through historic analysis we have found that valuation multiple ranges are commonly 20% to 25% on each side of what would be considered fair value. This is another indication that the markets are not as efficient as academia may represent.

In order to focus on the fundamental results of the company, price targets should be reassessed at each quarterly earnings release and on any significant news. Price targets are not set and forgotten; the actual hope is that each quarter the company is outperforming your expectations and you feel justified in increasing your price target channel. Continuing with the Nike example, you can see in Figure 9.5 that price targets were first set in 2009. As time progressed, price targets were increased due to

FIGURE 9.5   Nike equity price and price target channel 2008 to October 2019

continued growth in sales and margins. For about four years from 2009 to 2013, the stock stayed within the channel and would be a comfortable hold in the portfolio.

In 2013 Nike started to push valuation boundaries. Potentially you may still hold the stock, but it would become less comfortable and a lower NAV size in the portfolio would be appropriate. In 2014, the stock really pushed valuation boundaries and broke out of the area where it would be expected to create outperformance. This was caused by very significant multiple expansion without any real change in fundamentals or expectations for the business. In October 2019, the stock, although still a great long-term company, is simply being traded at valuation levels that don't make sense in the realm of expecting a return compensating for the risk. In Figure 9.6, the EV/EBITDA multiple is added to the analysis.

The double line is the EV/EBITDA multiple with the axis on the right. From 2009 to 2019, Nike's EV/EBITDA multiple increased from ten times to close to 25 times EBITDA. This multiple expansion was primarily driven by central banks lowering rates causing investors to move from bonds to equities, because they could not reach return expectations with the low bond yields. In moving capital into the equity markets, they naturally wanted to be as safe as possible, so they flocked to what were considered stable margin companies (Nike, McDonalds, Coca-Cola, etc.). Stable margin companies actually became momentum companies due to the demand created by low rates. Unfortunately, holding Nike in 2015 with the multiple above 16 times EBITDA, the risk return was no longer sufficient to warrant an investment. Future expansion of cash flows were priced in and there was certainly nothing contrarian about it.

FIGURE 9.6   Nike equity price and price target channel *plus EV/EBITDA multiple* 2008
to October 2019

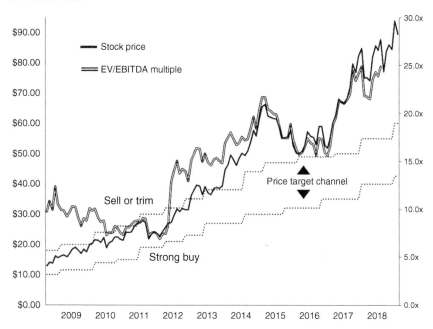

Using the same discounted owner's cash flow analysis and expectations, we can
calculate the markets *expected or discounted* growth in cash flows over the next seven
years. Nike grew owner's cash flows from 2014 to 2019 by 6.5% annually, which was
actually less than our estimates in 2013, so the stock went up while underperforming
our expectations. We would now forecast 7% future cash flow growth, because we
still like the company and are willing to project above the recent historic growth.
Using the investment hurdle and backing into the market implied growth rate for
Nike today shows a 15% annual cash flow growth rate expectation for seven years.
That is simply not going to happen. What the market is actually doing is accepting
a much lower rate of return to be an equity holder of Nike stock. Should you accept
a projected return of only 50 basis points above an investment grade bond (paying
24 times EV/EBITDA) to hold equity in a company that, however great, has a cyclical
nature and operates in a sporting goods market that is mature? Over time, that type
of investment is not going to outperform or create solid absolute returns.

Superior business models are the sign of a great company and valuation will not
help in finding *who* has the best business model. Valuation is the answer to *when* and
how much a manager should invest in a superior business to achieve outperformance.

CHAPTER 10

CAPITAL ALLOCATION

- *Capital expenditures (capex) and research and development (R&D)*
- *Acquisitions and corporate strategy*
- *Stock buybacks, dividends, and debt pay down*
- *Return on equity of new investments: First priority*

As you think about the owner's yield valuation methodology, it may come to mind that the future forecasting portion will be very dependent on management's capital allocation of the cash that is being created. There is no point in creating cash if it is not managed and allocated well. Capital allocation is one of the key areas that should be focused on when first interacting with management teams. Analyzing capital allocation decisions, the return on future projects, and management's execution on the future projects should be a high priority.

One of the more interesting ways to judge management is in listening to their thought process on where cash will be allocated. Capital expenditures, R&D (which may be expensed, but is a nonoperating use of cash), M&A, stock buybacks, dividends, and debt pay down are the options, and understanding how management thinks about these options can be a valuable learning process for an investor.

Capital expenditures (capex) and research and development (R&D)

Capex decisions are often the most important decisions a company makes each year and all capex is not equal. Thinking about what is maintenance capex and what portion is truly growing the business helps you understand the business and its potential.

A theme park that spends millions of dollars on a new roller coaster might seem to be adding a new long-term asset and growing the business. However, when you recognize they build a new roller coaster every two years and grow at only 4%, you may view the capex differently. What would happen if they did not build and advertise a new roller coaster every other year? The roller coaster may be functional for 20 years, but if it only drives attendance for two years, how quickly should it be depreciated from a true business cash flow perspective? These new rollercoasters are needed every two years to maintain the owner's cash flows you are counting on. Redrafting the income statement to depreciate roller coasters over five years as opposed to 20 years will drastically change the net income and earnings per share (EPS) of the company.

On the flip side is research and development (R&D) that is expensed and is potentially truly adding to the future growth and value of the company. A company like Alphabet (Google) is an interesting example, because they make significant investments in their non-Google subsidiaries that do not produce profits or at least produce profits well below the margins and return on equity of the core Google franchise. Redrafting the income statement of Alphabet adding back non-core, nonprofit-producing expenses will show a much higher cash flow yield and EPS than is demonstrated in their current generally accepted accounting principles (GAAP) filings. In this case, Google may even be happy with the conservative nature of GAAP accounting, because it hides the true earnings of their core Google business and the dominance of their franchise from regulators who have started to become worried about the power they wield on the web.

GAAP accounting standards are determined by a respected group of accountants with the explicit goal of creating accounting standards that provide consistency and uniformity across all businesses. The accounting board does a great job with this consistency mandate to fairly communicate financial results and balance sheet items, but it is impossible to take into account all the nuances of every different type of company. GAAP accounting is a place to start, but an investor should really think about the business and redraft the financial statements to draw the most accurate picture of business reality. This is a very important skill set and process in due diligence and takes time and experience to perform well. It is one of the key reasons the markets are still inefficient. GAAP accounting will evolve, but the mandate of consistency and uniformity across all businesses will never allow for the very best financial picture and analysis of any one singular business. Investors that understand, and consider in valuation, accounting nuances will have an information advantage.

Acquisitions and corporate strategy

As the US economy matures, acquisitions have become a bigger and bigger part of corporate strategy. Acquisition activity (mergers and acquisitions; M&A) is cyclical, but it is in an upward trend. In Figure 10.1, the solid bars and left-hand vertical axis represent M&A transactions since 1985. We are in the third wave of M&A transactions since 1985. There have been 111,000 M&A transactions since 2010 (post–financial crisis), the largest number ever recorded. The horizontal black line is the number of public companies in the US over $250 million in market cap, which peaked at about 8,000 in 1997. The current total is about 4,000 publicly held companies, which is a 50% drop in the last 20 years. This is a result of the high M&A activity, but it is also a result of the growth in private equity assets. More and more companies are choosing to go private and more are remaining private longer, as we discussed in a prior chapter.

FIGURE 10.1   Number of M&A transactions and number of US publicly listed companies 1985 to 2018

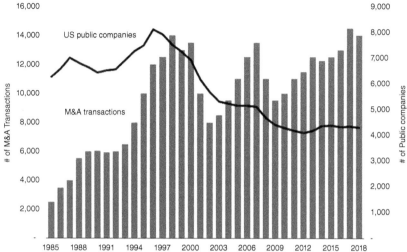

To the public equity investor this creates two concerns. The first is obvious: the universe of potential investments is shrinking, hence creating fewer options. Fewer options will create more efficiency in the markets on the margin. The second issue is probably more important and that is your public company's competitors and industry disruptors may very well be privately held. Privately held companies are harder to perform due diligence on and understand their effect on the competitive environment. Additionally, they may be private to allow a strategic focus on growth over profits, which would be harder to accomplish as a public company more subject to minority shareholder demands. This makes them more willing to embrace strategies that are extremely price competitive or disruptive. Competition is ubiquitous in corporate America, but some competition is mature and rational and some is disruptive.

If you are competing against a company that does not have the same constraints as you do, your business is being disrupted. When a venture capital company backs your competitor with large amounts of cash and tells them to grow at 100+% a year, you are in a disruptive competitive environment. This may sound like a crazy strategy for the VC-backed company, but it is not. VC firms expect many companies to be complete losses, so they are looking for a few to be very big winners of 100+ times their initial investment. So in today's environment, due diligence of both the public and private companies in the industry and those companies that may be entering the industry from other industries must be performed. The days of looking at the public company comparable set of companies and considering that the competitive environment are over.

From a use of cash perspective, almost all companies are now looking at acquisitions continually and thinking about how they can fit strategically with their goals. Some are more aggressive than others, but everyone is looking. If public disclosure and greater public scrutiny is a negative to being public, a major positive is having a secondary liquid currency to use for acquisitions in the form of your public stock. Understanding the thought process from management about acquisitions can lead to a better understanding of management's true motivations:

- Are they looking to be empire builders?
- Are they looking to expand outside their current industry?
- What hurdle rates do they use to value acquisitions?
- Are they acquiring to grow or out of fear of competition?

When a company opens the door to acquisitions the range of options is enormous and understanding how the management team defines this range of options is key. This is the investor's cash flow being spent, so investors and management must feel aligned in their goals. Acquisitions can make or break companies very quickly and a number of studies have found success rates to be in the sub-50% range historically. To be a long-term investor, one must have trust and belief in the management team's M&A strategy.

Stock buybacks, dividends, and debt pay-down

Cash flows can be returned to shareholders through stock buybacks, dividends, and the paying down of debt. There is often debate about which is the best course of action. In answering that question, the first decision should be determining an optimal debt level for the company. The optimal debt level is a subjective decision made by the company board and is a window into how the board thinks. There is no right answer, but it can be enlightening to understand the level of risk the management team is comfortable taking on.

Once the optimal debt level is set, cash flow should go first to paying down debt if it is above the optimal level. Once debt levels are where they are desired, the debate should focus on dividends or stock buybacks. Given that shareholders have different views on this debate, many companies choose to do a little of both. Dividends put the cash back in the hands of the shareholder, which gives an investor control, but also creates reinvestment risk and is generally tax disadvantaged. Stock buybacks put money back into the hands of the shareholders by making their shares worth more as the overall number of shares decreases. Stock buybacks have been a large driver of the markets in the 2010s, because cash flows have been strong and buybacks have been embraced by management teams. Figure 10.2 illustrates the massive buyback activity that has occurred since 2010. More than 17% of the available shares in the market were purchased through company buybacks in

FIGURE 10.2   S&P 500 trailing 12-month net stock buyback activity 1998 to October 2019

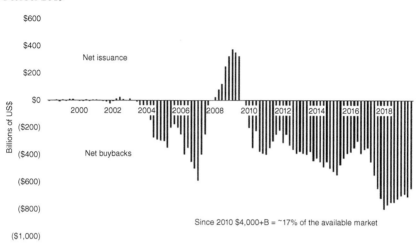

the 2010s. This level of stock buyback activity is significantly above any other time in history.

Although buybacks often seem to be a great indicator of success, because the company has created cash flow and is signaling they are confident in the future by buying their shares, there are a few concerns. One would think the timing of company buyback purchases would be managed better than the timing of any outside investment manager, because the management team knows the company better than anybody else. Unfortunately, the history of stock buybacks is not very compelling. On average, companies have a track record of buying back stock at high valuations and issuing stock during times of stress at low valuations. To be fair, management might like to buy back shares during times of stress, but is unable due to cash flow and balance sheet constraints.

Additionally, there can be conflicts of interest as management compensation may be based on earnings per share (EPS) growth. Buybacks help management achieve their EPS compensation milestones. Even if earnings remain flat, if 10% of the stock was repurchased then EPS grew 10%. In the 2010s, simply monitoring EPS could be misleading, because companies bought back stock and received a healthy tax cut in 2017. The combination could make a declining company look like a growing company if only earnings per share were monitored.

Stock option compensation plans are also a concern. Shares being bought back may be going right back out to the executives of the company, so there is no value being created for the shareholders. Investors need to focus on the net shares repurchased, not just the buyback amount.

Return on equity of new investments: First priority

It should always be remembered that the best capital allocation use is investing in growth projects with high return on equity. For all the reasons noted on superior business models previously, what you would like to see most are CEOs who believe they have future projects that warrant capital and will enhance the company's return on equity by growing revenues or leveraging expenses. Capital going back into projects with growth sustainability to produce future cash flows should always be the first priority. An investor should love to hear that the company is not buying back stock or issuing dividends, because it has so many compelling high return-on-equity projects that need capital.

CHAPTER 11

PORTFOLIO MANAGEMENT

- *Portfolio construction: Top down*
- *Portfolio construction: Bottom up*
- *Gross and net exposures*
- *Market timing*
- *Portfolio risk*
- *Equity factors and your portfolio*
- *Volatility and behavioral mistakes*
- *Managing individual portfolio positions*
- *Portfolio rebalancing*
- *Conviction and portfolio management*
- *Managing individual portfolio positions and behavioral pitfalls*
- *Trading*
- *Options*

Portfolio management methodologies are under-analyzed and underrated in their contribution to creating outperformance. Similar to security selection, portfolio management is half science and half art. The science is in the analysis of construction, liquidity, volatility, and trading execution. The art is heavily influenced by understanding one's own risk tolerance levels and behavioral biases. Everyone falls prey to behavioral mistakes and, unfortunately, it is a problem that never completely goes away. With experience a portfolio manager can keep mistakes to a minimum, but no one completely overcomes behavioral and psychological pitfalls. Experience and process are the only methods of learning and becoming a better portfolio manager.

Portfolio construction: Top down

Constructing a portfolio is the culmination of your initial firm strategy vision and all your security selection work. The goals of the strategy need to be clear and in focus as the portfolio is constructed. Specific security selection will ultimately enable you to build your expectations for the portfolio from the bottom up, but first let's look at the thought process from the top down. The top-down thought process can create a general structure that can then be tweaked for the specific securities that are compelling at different times.

Each individual investment has the characteristics of potential return, volatility, and correlation. The firm's strategy-defined alpha and volatility goals will dictate optimal concentration levels. For simplicity, we are assuming relatively equal weighting, because any portfolio can have a long tail of securities in the portfolio that does not have much effect on results. The number of positions that account for 80+% of the portfolio net asset value (NAV) is the focus here. Managers often fall into two camps: those who are very concerned about volatility and diversify to a point that they may not have an opportunity for alpha creation or those who concentrate and are willing to accept a high level of volatility. Accepting a high level of volatility will offer the opportunity to create superior returns, but it will also put stress on portfolio managers and their ability to keep behavioral mistakes to a minimum. The thought process in determining the optimal concentration levels for a strategy is outlined in Figure 11.1. The keys are to understand your universe of potential investments and define your goals.

The combination of the strategy universe and alpha goal will define optimal concentration, but then security selection win/loss rate will be the major factor

FIGURE 11.1   Concentration, risk, and alpha analysis

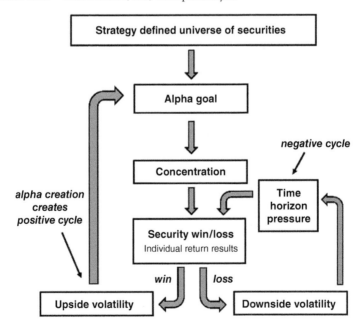

determining returns. Higher concentration (fewer companies) should increase a manager's potential win/loss rate success to a point; deeper research on fewer companies makes for better decisions. The relationship can only go so far and is dependent on process, strategy, and team issues. Win/loss rate may improve by dropping from a 50-company portfolio to a 20-company portfolio, but there is going to be little difference in win/loss rate if you drop from 20 companies to a 5-company portfolio.

A concentrated portfolio pressures the portfolio win/loss rate and gives a manager the opportunity to achieve upside volatility in earnings, which if done consistently is alpha and creates a positive cycle in the investment process. This is the scenario you want, but recognize that win/loss rate is volatile (even for good managers) and there will be periods of downside volatility. Downside volatility brings time horizon pressure into the outcomes. If the win/loss rate is great, then no one really cares about time horizon, but when win/loss rates drop and downside volatility occurs time horizon becomes an issue, as pressure to succeed heightens. Limited partners (clients) become concerned, managers and staff become frustrated, and the pressure to produce positive returns can create a negative cycle detrimental to returns.

> *We always have focused on concentration; we want to have concentrated portfolios of the very best ideas.*
>
> —*Mark Mobius, investor*

The optimal number of positions in a portfolio varies. If you have a big team and run a global portfolio, you may be able to add diversification benefits well beyond 25 positions. We can get very quantitative with this type of analysis, but simply think about the fact that there are about 25 countries with accessible, liquid markets and there are ten sectors and there are three market cap levels. If you have one company from each of those relatively unique universes, you would have 750 companies (25 country × 10 sector × 3 cap). At 750 positions, even globally, little diversification benefit is being added at the end, but you are clearly still adding diversification benefit beyond 25 positions. One way to think about this is from a percentage of the defined universe perspective. One strategy may look at the US Russell 1000 as the universe; 25 stocks is 2.5 % of the universe. A US Russell 3000 universe strategy would hold 75 stocks at 2.5%. The relationship is not linear, but a percentage of the universe is a better way to think about the number of positions held than an absolute number that is expected to fit all strategies.

The schematic in Figure 11.2 illustrates the portfolio relationships. Alpha potential, volatility, and win/loss rate all move higher as the number of positions is decreased. However, they all have different slopes and limits to the value they can add. If you hold one stock, your alpha potential and volatility are at maximum limits, but your win/loss rate is under maximum pressure. In defining your optimal number of positions level, you have to assume some reasonable win/loss rate and then prioritize alpha or volatility (risk).

FIGURE 11.2 Diversification, alpha, volatility, and win/loss relationships

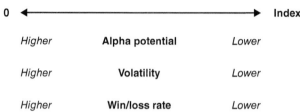

No investor can have everything, and it is a mistake to assume you will produce a win/loss rate that is incredible. The strategy needs to make a decision to prioritize alpha or volatility. This book has been primarily focused on alpha, so let's look at alpha prioritization in a few scenarios.

The US large cap market is the most efficient equity market in the world and your diversification benefits drop significantly at 20 positions, which is where Buffett's original analysis was focused. The firm's alpha goal is very important. If you follow Buffett's philosophy of 20 to 25 sector diversified positions and you have an alpha goal of 1,000 basis points, you are going to fail (unless you assume some incredible win/loss rate). To reach alpha potential of 1,000 basis points in the US large cap universe, you will need to push the concentration level below 20 to 25 positions to 8 to 12 positions. Holding an average of ten positions over time puts significant pressure on your security selection and time horizon to reach 1,000 basis points of alpha. In reality, 1,000 basis points of alpha in a long-only US large cap strategy is not likely to be a repeatable and sustainable goal. The universe is simply too efficient. Getting all the pieces in place for an alpha-focused US large cap fund would look something like an alpha goal of 500+ basis points with 10 to15 positions resulting in an average volatility of approximately 20 and a good, but reasonable, win/loss rate.

Once the concentration level is determined to achieve your alpha goal, it is important to understand the volatility and time horizon that will be a result of the concentration decision. The resulting volatility and time horizon have to be understood and accepted by the investor base or the strategy will not be able to be executed. A strategy and investor base mismatch is very common and one of the top reasons for firms' failing. In almost all issues associated with active investing, the key is the correct alignment of the different pieces of the strategy and process.

In summary, portfolio concentration hinges on doing the following:

- Making a prioritization choice of alpha or volatility
- Aligning the resulting factors (alpha, volatility, time horizon) to achieve firm goals
- Articulating and then attracting an investor base that understands the implications of the concentration decision

Portfolio construction: Bottom up

Although a general portfolio structure has been designed, the precise individual position NAV levels and sector weightings have to be driven from the bottom up. When performing security selection, the very best individual company opportunities should be selected based on all the fundamentals of future growth, competitive environment, operating leverage, and valuation. This selection process cannot be overridden to fit a portfolio structure. The portfolio structure has to be flexible enough to accommodate the fact that at different times in history there will be different investment opportunity sets. When the focus shifts from security selection to portfolio construction, the investments selected should be thought of from the perspective of expected return, risk, and correlation. The focus becomes what the selected companies can provide as a group from a return perspective and how this group will act in different market environments from a risk perspective.

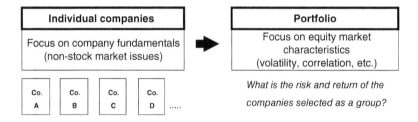

At this point, there is always some struggle between top-down and bottom-up decision-making and which takes precedence. Specific individual company (bottom-up) opportunities will be very different in different market environments. At certain times, there may be a large number of compelling high-risk positions and at other times core stable compounders may have higher than normal expected returns. The only way to reconcile a top-down structure that meets strategic goals with the individual companies that seem compelling in that market environment is to stay flexible and find a balance.

Gross and net exposures

As a portfolio comes together, **gross and net exposures** are a focus. Many long-only fund managers do not have this additional issue, because they have a mandate to maintain exposure levels at a certain level. Often long-only funds are providing some form of beta exposure to a certain market, and their investors want to maintain exposure at or near 100% at all times. The investors are still looking for alpha, but they do not want leverage or market timing to be options that the manager has to deploy.

For hedge fund managers, the primary focus is centered on these questions:

- What is the optimal **net** and **gross exposure** level for the portfolio?
- Do you attempt to try and time the market by moving exposures up and down?

After analyzing optimal net exposure levels for a long/short equity hedge fund, I believe the original Alfred Winslow Jones model of 100% long and 50% short is optimal. There is no exact quantitative reasoning for this belief. Generally it stems from trying to strike a balance between two major goals of a hedge fund: *overall performance* and *performance in down markets*.

Overall performance recognizes the fact that markets will go up over time, so to be completely market neutral gives up some return that may not be necessary. The second is the goal of producing absolute positive returns. Managing a portfolio 100% long by 50% short offers a chance to hedge and produce positive returns in a down market, while at the same time being able to capture some of the natural market beta that is available. It is also a recognition that long returns will always be greater than short returns over time. Issues of shorting are discussed in chapter 12. If the emphasis were on trying to always produce absolute returns in any market (a tough goal), the portfolio would have to be managed in the 100% long by 70% short range or 30% net exposure.

The 100% long and 50% short exposure level also recognizes that significant leverage is problematic. A manager could get to 50% net exposure by being 200% long and 150% short. In an equity hedge fund when gross exposure gets much over 250%, the volatility of the portfolio on a daily and monthly basis gets extreme enough that it causes behavioral mistakes in most managers.

Alpha on the long and short side in any concentrated portfolio will be volatile on a monthly basis. In a down market of 5%, if you are running 200% long and 150% short and underperform that month by negative 500 basis points in both your short and long portfolios, the outcome may be a larger drawdown than the firm and its investors can manage.

Example: Down 5.0% market (beta) monthly return with 500 bps negative excess return

Exposure	Return	Contribution
200% gross long exposure	−5.0% (beta) plus -500bps (excess return)	−20.0%
150% gross short exposure	+5.0% (beta) plus -500bps (excess return)	0.0%
	Gross monthly return	−20.0%

A negative 20% month can force bad decisions by the portfolio manager or even stress the longevity of the firm. When issues such as the longevity of the firm arise, behavioral mistakes occur compounding an already difficult time. There is no exact answer, but doing scenario analyses on different exposure levels and potential outcomes and considering what level of drawdowns the firm can handle without too much stress is important to understanding leverage limits.

> *Leverage magnifies outcomes but doesn't add value.*
>
> —*Howard Marks, investor*

Significant leverage is not needed to meet the 1,000 basis point alpha goal we have been discussing. Excessive leverage can create the occurrence of a negative feedback loop forcing early exits from positions and most likely getting whipsawed back and forth by the market. When managers feel like they need significant leverage to accomplish their goals they should first question their strategy or ability to provide value through security selection. The other potential reason for managers to use significant leverage is they may not have goal congruence with the allocator and are taking on high risk in the hope of receiving a big compensation year from their 20% performance fee. The easiest way to avoid this issue and ensure goal congruence is to make sure managers have the vast majority of their own money in the fund being managed identically to clients. A hedge fund can be designed as free optionality for managers if allocators do not emphasize issues like managers' personal financial involvement and the financial involvement of their friends and family.

> *Using leverage is like playing Russian roulette. It means that you are inevitably going to get a bullet in the head.*
>
> —*Ray Dalio, investor*

Market timing

As clarification, moving exposures up or down more than 5% (even for a short time period) is market timing. The value (or destruction of value) in moving exposure up and down for different reasons is much debated. Many successful managers, such as Peter Lynch in the following quote, might call for no market timing decisions, because they have seen too many managers err on their timing call and lose money. It would be easy to state that market timing is a bad idea and move on to the next issue.

> *Trying to predict the direction of the market over one year, or even two years, is impossible.*
>
> —*Peter Lynch*

But moving exposures in some limited, systematic form can add value over time. The desire to change exposures can come from either bottom-up analysis or top-down issues. There may be times when managers simply feel they have a great long portfolio at this point in time for company-specific reasons and want to maintain higher gross long exposure. From a top-down perspective, there may be times when increased caution is warranted due to large macro or general equity market issues. The caveat to the concept of market timing is that it is very difficult and these "period-in-time" opinions on a great long portfolio or time for additional caution driven by macro events can either be wrong or take a long time to occur. When exposures are moved too far from the base, portfolio managers can be caught off-balance and significantly hurt returns moving exposures back and forth.

Significant exposure moves in short periods of time are a bad idea. Moving exposures in a controlled fashion over intermediate periods (six months to two years) can be alpha enhancing. To illustrate this issue, I have defined an exposure structure in Figure 11.3 that I think can be productive. The most important thing is for a manager to have considered when, why, and how much exposures will change in advance. Trying to make significant exposure decisions in the midst of market stress is a mistake.

This structure tries to define the incremental exposure moves a manager might make and an idea of how often variances from a base might occur. These are intermediate term (one- to three-year) market biases and use 50% net long as a baseline. Making exposure changes beyond these incremental levels can be a recipe for destroying security selection research through poor portfolio management. This type of exposure range gives managers an opportunity to express their views on the market environment without allowing a bad market timing call to cause major problems throughout the portfolio. One of the reasons to allow some flexibility is that markets have major drawdowns every seven years on average and those drawdowns are a great opportunity to make money from a long perspective.

No one will ever call the bottom exactly, but if you allow long exposure to move up slowly as the market is in the midst of a major drawdown, you should be rewarded. During a 20+% market drawdown it can also be difficult to find shorts that are compelling and this enables a manager to take off some short exposure. When a market

FIGURE 11.3   Exposure limit structure

Net exposure (%)	Market state	Probability
75	Extreme bullishness	maybe 1× per decade
60	1–2 standard deviations cheap	~ 20% of the time
50	Steady state	~ 60% of the time
40	1–2 standard deviations expensive	~ 20% of the time
25	Extreme bearishness	maybe 1× per decade

does trough, stocks that are commonly attractive short candidates, such as cyclical and levered companies, can have very vicious upward moves as investors race to buy back into the market. The following 6 to 12 months after a market bottom are usually led by what many would call "junk" companies, those with leverage and volatile margins. In most other environments, companies with leverage and volatile margins are good short candidates, so slowly bringing short exposure down in significant market drawdowns can make sense.

Portfolio risk

From an academic perspective, risk is volatility, the standard deviation of a portfolio's returns. Choosing some singular quantitative measure for risk is necessary to perform quantitative financial portfolio analysis, which is useful. However, one number or a historic graph cannot really define risk. Risk is made up of many factors. Volatility has to be experienced to be understood. A manager can understand what a volatility of 12 or 16 or 20 means only as they feel it and then analyze its effect on their portfolio management retrospectively.

Monitoring volatility can help managers understand how the market views the companies in their portfolio. All the work in deciding to invest has been on company fundamentals and future expectations, but the market can treat companies very differently from a trading volume and volatility perspective. It would be expected that a company with a high valuation would be more volatile due to the reliance on the future cash flow stream that is more unknown than more mature stable companies. Individual company volatility can vary greatly. Two stocks that are both valued at 50 times P/E do not necessarily trade the same way. Figure 11.4 shows the historic volatility of three well-known companies. You can see that each one has a wide range of volatility based on the market sentiment of the day.

Portfolio managers need to acknowledge the wide range of potential volatility and consider how to size each of the positions in the portfolio. An investor would never want to hold Netflix if they thought it had the same potential return as Johnson & Johnson. However if Netflix had an expected annual return of 25% over the next four years and Johnson & Johnson's expected return was 7% from a risk/return perspective the risk may be considered equivalent. Some form of a return per unit of risk analysis, whether it be a Sharpe ratio, defined as the return minus the risk free rate divided by the volatility of the excess return, or some other similar metric, should be routinely performed and monitored to aid in the overall risk analysis.

Would you size positions equivalently if they have the same risk/reward ratio?

Although it may seem that optimizing for a return per unit of risk metric is the best methodology and should be strictly adhered to in the portfolio construction process, every analysis has drawbacks.

The Sharpe ratio drawback, when it is used to determine the NAV size in a portfolio, is that it assumes investment returns are normally distributed. Investment returns

FIGURE 11.4 Historic volatility of S&P 500, Johnson & Johnson, Goldman Sachs, and Netflix

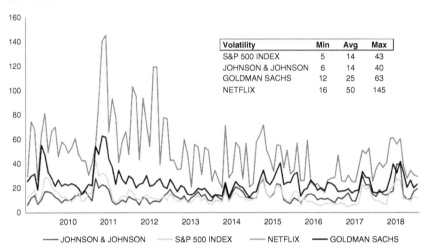

are *not* normally distributed, there are many outliers. This assumption will generally make lower risk (less volatile) investments look more attractive. The reason for this is the volatility of the security is calculated historically and the return is a forecasted expectation. In the scenario in the previous paragraph, we calculated that Johnson & Johnson and Netflix have average volatilities of 14 and 50, respectively. It is relatively easy to be comfortable projecting a 10% annual return for Johnson & Johnson. The equivalent for Netflix would be approximately 35%, which is a large enough number that it becomes harder to take comfort in the projection.

Psychologically it is hard to predict outlier returns, even though we know they have existed in the past and will in the future. For this reason, a strict process built completely on return per unit of risk will result in constructing lower-risk portfolios and lower-risk security selection. This may not result in the optimal result, because the portfolio may not hold enough risk. This may seem like a strange statement—"not enough risk"—but risk allows higher returns and alpha creation. Risk has to be understood and not accepted without compensatory potential returns, but the lowest risk portfolio is not the optimal portfolio.

Return per unit of risk is a compelling consideration, but there is no one correct answer. NAV weighting comes down to your conviction in each position and the position's relationship (characteristics and correlation) to the other positions in the portfolio. One strategy that some portfolio managers believe in, and I have seen be successful, is a barbell approach. On one end, very-high-risk positions that are believed to have great return potential and could be those outlier positive returns. On the other end, very stable positions that should help maintain some portfolio stability in a drawdown. The stability creates balance, so a manager is not forced into mistakes during extreme volatility.

> *[Success comes from] preservation of capital and home runs.*
> —George Soros, investor

This is all contingent on what type of companies are being found in your security selection process, because again you want to have a top-down structure, but building bottom up is important so you don't force poor investments into the portfolio due to an inflexible portfolio management structure.

Historic volatility is great for past attribution and can be one indicator of future risk, but understanding risk has to be done holistically. To understand risk it is necessary to look at the portfolio through every risk lens available. Many managers focus on beta, the level of volatility in relation to the market, but it is, once again, a single historic indicator. Calculating the two-year historic beta of all the stocks in a portfolio and applying an NAV weight is the current beta of the portfolio, but it can be very misleading, especially in good market environments and in the small cap universe. Individual company betas are volatile and can be quite low during stable upward markets but then become very volatile in a market drawdown. It is more important to understand the type of position you have from a fundamental perspective and how it will perform in different markets than be a slave to the historic quantitative outputs.

A small cap, levered hotel company may have a beta of 1.0 or even below 1.0 for years, but when a recession occurs it will become a high beta stock. Any levered, cyclically oriented company is not a low risk stock regardless of what the past few years may demonstrate quantitatively. It is more informative to group all the stocks in a portfolio by level of cyclicality, variance of operating margins, and balance sheet leverage and assign the different groups *expected* betas to determine a future expected beta of the portfolio. Companies have unique balance sheet and operating margin business models that can look very different from a risk perspective in different market environments. True risk is inherent to a business model and balance sheet structure.

Correlations are similar to betas. They are important to analyze and understand but can be very volatile. Stocks may act in an uncorrelated manner for years, but if they have the same business model characteristics and business drivers, they will be correlated over longer periods or in times of stress. It is, again, better to understand the company and determine the future correlation to other companies based on business model similarities. *Analyze history but not only recent history.*

Illiquidity is always a risk factor that should be considered. Again, historic analysis is great, but markets can dry up quickly in times of stress. It is a good practice to not only look at the past few years' liquidity metrics but also what kind of liquidity existed in bad market environments. Illiquidity metrics should always be communicated to investors so they have an understanding of their liquidity options.

Stress testing a portfolio with different historic and anticipated scenarios is a good exercise to perform on a regular basis. These scenarios should coincide with the risks found in company due diligence and cited in the investment thesis. Historic interest rate, oil, or currency crises scenarios should be reviewed, but in a concentrated portfolio very unusual, eclectic events can stress the portfolio, so customize the scenarios.

- If the portfolio is heavily weighted to a few retailers, what is the drawdown risk associated with Amazon entering their industry?
- If the portfolio holds a number of health care names, how will it act with government regulatory change scenarios?

The best practice in risk analysis is to use as many different quantitative metrics and qualitative scenarios as possible to get a full picture of the risk profile. Risk analysis, similar to security due diligence, is a mosaic. Points of view from many different perspectives offers the clearest picture.

There is no way to construct a concentrated, alpha-driven portfolio without significant risk factors. The key is to understand the risk implications of the portfolio that are created from the individual security selection. It should be recognized that, although risk is often considered bad or something to be limited, risk is necessary to achieve alpha. Taking on the right risks is positive and should not be limited. The question becomes, "Is this a risk that can be accepted?"

Equity factors and your portfolio

Factors have become a constant topic of conversation in the investment industry over the last five years, but they have been analyzed and discussed in academia for many years. The growth in passive investing has brought factors into mainstream discussions, because passive diversified portfolios are driven by factors, not individual company selection. Entire books have been written on factors, so view this as a simple introduction into their effect on portfolios and risk. For a more complete analysis of factors, the Fama/French website managed by the Dartmouth Tuck School of Business is a very good resource (https://famafrench.dimensional.com/).

Factors are specific drivers of market performance and may be macroeconomic or style in nature. Fundamental investors are primarily interested in style factors, which are company and stock market metrics. At the core, factor portfolio construction is simply screening and ranking companies by certain stock attributes and choosing some subset to invest in with the expectation of enhanced returns and an expected volatility.

For a concentrated active investment manager, they can be used to analyze a portfolio to understand the potential influence on returns. They can also be used for the attribution of past returns. It is very possible to outperform the general market over a period of time, but in a factor attribution analysis realize that all the outperformance came from a single factor bias and was not security specific outperformance. A value manager may outperform the market for a given year by 3.0%, but in a factor attribution analysis see that a portfolio of all value stocks outperformed the market by 3.0%, so in fact individual security selection added no value in their outperformance.

The specific definitions of each factor can vary by firm, but a very simple overview follows.

Factor	Description
Value	Value was originally defined by price-to-book ratio. Various other metrics may be used, but the general idea is to rank stocks by their relative valuation.
Momentum	Momentum is price change.
	Price change may be shorter term (90 days) or longer term (one year)
Quality	Quality is a combination of financial metrics, including return on equity, gross margin, operating margin stability, and balance sheet leverage.
Growth	Growth may be defined by sales or earnings growth depending on the specific firm creating the factor.

Momentum is probably the most important factor from a risk perspective, because momentum stocks can be quite volatile. Momentum can also be quite frustrating, because it can take stocks to valuation levels that you never thought were possible. This can lead to concerns over having sold too early and is especially problematic in short investing. Although momentum is a factor that should be understood from a risk perspective in a portfolio, it does not mean that you would prefer to avoid all stocks with momentum. A portfolio with no stocks demonstrating positive momentum can cause a lot of frustration in upward trending markets. A portfolio with a low or negative momentum bias may have less downside risk over time; however, in the short term it can be the cause of underperformance. As mentioned, there is no right answer, but factors are another way to view the portfolio and think about risk.

Volatility and behavioral mistakes

Portfolio volatility is a constant topic for managers. At certain times, volatility can become too dominant a focus in a firm or strategy. An interesting question to consider is,

If both the manager and the investor are willing to accept high volatility, have a long time horizon, and have conviction in their security selection should volatility be of any concern?

That would be a great environment to invest in, but the answer is still yes. High volatility creates human stress and human stress creates behavioral mistakes. The key is understanding volatility and its effects on decision-makers. Investing will always be volatile and stressful, but all portfolio managers need to understand their personal volatility tolerance.

At what point is volatility driving decisions, not fundamental analysis? Of course, we are usually talking about downside volatility, but even wild upside volatility can create greed and cause managers to cast off risk structures and make bad decisions. The old adage of the markets are either driven by fear or greed is very true and maintaining proper (pre-considered and analyzed) risk structures is important to stop from having fear or greed overwhelm rationality. Risk tolerance limits are personal for every portfolio manager and can be understood only through experience. Trial and error and the introspection to understand limits and mistakes are the ways to develop as a portfolio manager.

Reason must overcome emotion.

—Howard Marks, investor

Managing individual portfolio positions

When previously discussing exposure levels and concentration, we often assumed equal weight individual position sizes for simplicity purposes. Few managers equal weight their positions, because conviction in the outcome and risk of the individual positions are different. Making some positions larger and others smaller based on return, risk, and conviction makes sense. The exact structure employed for NAV position size is specific to a firm's alpha goals and risk limits. For illustrative purposes, Figure 11.5 is an example of a structure that I have seen be successful for concentrated equity managers.

FIGURE 11.5   Portfolio net asset value structure

Risk type	Base case NAV size	Min. NAV size	Max NAV at cost	Max NAV at value	Expected volatility	Expected return—1 yr
High conviction and low risk	10%	3%	10%	15%	< 20	15%
Low risk in cyclical industry	7%	3%	7%	12%	< 35	25%
High risk in stable industry	5%	3%	5%	8%	< 50	40%
High risk and high return	3%	1%	3%	5%	50 +	50+%

You can see that there is a wide range from 1% to 15%. When a position goes over 15%, the associated volatility will test many managers' risk tolerance limits. A 20% down month in the single 15% position will cost the portfolio 3.0%. If that single name is accompanied by a few other names in the portfolio (which is likely the case in these scenarios), the overall portfolio drawdown may be reaching levels of stress that may cause selling positions unnecessarily.

Concern over the level of a monthly drawdown should not be the cause for selling a position; selling a position should be driven by fundamental results not reaching the expectations in your investment thesis. Long time horizons are necessary to allow the investment thesis to play out, but everyone does look at monthly performance numbers. Short-term performance reviews are an unavoidable part of the investment management business, so create a portfolio structure that won't stress decisions or client relationships.

On the other end of the position size spectrum, holding a long tail of positions below 1% can be unproductive, because they will never have a material effect on the portfolio. Some managers like to add very small positions to the portfolio as a way to force analyst time to be allocated to the company. This feels too much like a "ready-fire-aim" mentality, but it may have merits in certain firms.

An additional factor is correlation among the portfolio positions. Stocks with very high correlation should often be thought of as one position from a risk perspective and potentially maintained at appropriate NAV levels. If a manager holds three chemical companies, it would probably be concerning to hold all three in one of the top NAV categories. It is the recognition of risk that is important. There is not a precise definitive level of exposure that is good or bad.

Where individual position NAV levels fall within these extremes is generally managed by expected return and risk. My personal process is defined by the price target channels discussed back in the chapter on valuation (chapter 9). A position may have a base case of 5% of NAV and fluctuate +/−2% based on where it sits within the price target channel and other market environment issues. Structure and process are important, because it forces scenario analysis before stress occurs

Portfolio rebalancing

Many investors consider portfolio rebalancing to be the second free lunch in investing, the first being diversification. Systematically selling small portions of the portfolios' winners to buy more of losing portfolio positions makes very intuitive sense and in many academic studies has been proven to add value. It especially adds value in more diversified portfolios by lowering risk. It ensures individual positions do not get too large and increase volatility. It, however, does not take into account the conviction levels of active management.

The struggle in the 2010s has been that portfolio rebalancing is a mean reversion concept. In the current central bank and disruption-driven market environment mean reversion has not worked well. If winners continue to win, rebalancing out of them is not productive.

What I have found works well for active managers with concentrated portfolios is to understand the growth and risk characteristics of each position and treat them differently. As an example, using the companies shown a few pages back in the volatility chart, assume the same level of conviction in each of the companies:

- Johnson & Johnson is a mature, low-growth, stable cash flow–producing company. It should be rebalanced back down consistently. Every time it hits the high end of a price target channel it should be sold materially. The reason is Johnson & Johnson is not a stock that is going to run away and provide a 300% return over the next few years. When it is partially sold, there is a high likelihood that it will not trade significantly higher. Even if the stock does not pull back to provide a better entry point, it can be bought back for a price not too far from where it was sold at a later date. In the reverse scenario, Johnson & Johnson should be a stock that is comfortable being bought when it is at the low end of its valuation level due to underperformance because of its stability.
- Netflix is a high-growth company and if the positive investment thesis is correct, it could be a big winner in the portfolio. In chapter 6 on strategy, we talked about first decile performance outperformers, and Netflix could be one of those outperformers. Johnson & Johnson can safely achieve performance above the fifth decile, but it won't be a first decile return–performing stock. Despite the volatility Netflix should be rebalanced less, because it has the potential to really drive outperformance. Netflix is also much harder to value than Johnson & Johnson, so there should be more room for error in the price targets (wider buy/sell range) and a less stringent selling policy. On the flip side, Netflix will be a company that should be bought very slowly during times of underperformance, because almost any stock that has the ability to achieve very high returns also has the ability to trade lower than anyone would expect. A 20% pullback may be a meaningful buying opportunity in Johnson & Johnson, but may not be in Netflix.

One of the important things I have learned from watching successful managers is that almost all held one or two companies with conviction for many years. These long-term winners drove a significant amount of outperformance and really made their firm successful. A single company that outperforms the index by more than 20% per year for 10 years can make a firm successful due to the outsized contribution. Continually rebalancing the position or significantly selling based on valuation will only hurt the contribution of these big winners. Early investors in Amazon, Domino's, Netflix, and a number of small and mid-cap technology companies produced ten-year annualized returns in excess of 30%. In an average year less than 5% of the US equity universe can boast of a ten-year annualized 20+% outperformance, so if you think you have a company like that you need to get the most out of it.

Replacement risk is another serious consideration when managing individual positions. If a portfolio manager continually exits positions after 20% short-term gains, there is a risk that finding another good company to invest in will take time. The new company may not be as good an opportunity as the company that went up 20%, despite the fact that the manager may feel the valuation is high on the original stock. Extremely high valuations are problematic, but slightly high valuations can cause selling that creates replacement risk.

Conviction and portfolio management

Conviction is one of the most important elements in active equity investing. It generally pertains to having belief in the companies you are invested in, so that you may buy more when they are down. Buying when a stock is down, which is both showing conviction in your research and being contrarian, adds value over time to the *buy and hold* annual return of your investment. If you remember from chapter 6, the probabilities of stock picking your way to 1,000 bps of alpha based on simple buy and hold returns are low. Being able to add exposure when a stock is down will add materially to outperformance.

> *The stock market demands conviction as surely as it victimises the unconvinced.*
> —*Peter Lynch, investor*

Conviction is mentioned in almost every active investment management book, but it is much easier to articulate on paper than execute. Significant drawdowns in stocks do not occur for no reason; there is almost always a very real issue occurring that might change your original investment thesis. The debate will center on two issues: is your investment thesis simply wrong, and has the time horizon been changed enough to lower the return significantly?

Active investing conviction is like confidence in sports. Any athlete knows playing with confidence is integral to success. Does telling an athlete to play with confidence right before a game add any value? Probably not. Confidence is built well before the game during practice. Practice creates belief in one's self. In athletics, repetition after repetition builds confidence. The same concept is true for investing: research due diligence and analysis before the stressful event is the only way to invest with conviction. *So telling someone to have conviction may help less than telling someone to do his or her work before stressful events occur.*

Managing individual portfolio positions and behavioral pitfalls

The most difficult issue in managing individual positions is understanding and trying to combat behavioral pitfalls. The problems are common and numerous and no one completely avoids them. Following are a few of the key issues.

- **Herding—following the investment crowd**

  Herding is one of the most common and destructive behavioral mistakes. In an industry where 70% is a very good win/loss rate, it is easy for people to question themselves. There is no obvious answer on what the future holds, so we can be easily swayed by the opinion of others. Herding often drives market cycles and bubbles, but it can also affect investment idea generation and due diligence. It is easier to talk to someone and listen to their story about a stock than do time-consuming due diligence. It would be very easy to avoid herding, if trends did not last so long, but they often do. In hot upward trending markets, momentum rules and herding looks like a great idea. Unfortunately no one knows when it will end and the end can be very fast and painful.

  > *Even the intelligent investor is likely to need considerable will power to keep from following the crowd.*
  >
  > —*Ben Graham, investor*

- **Selling winners—seeking the pride of a job well done; booking a win**

  It is a great feeling to have invested in a company and have the stock go up 50% and reach your initial price target. You forecasted the future and were correct. Selling the investment is the culmination of a positive event. When does the desire for this feeling overwhelm the fundamental analysis? Reinvestment risk is very real. Can you find another company as good as the one you are selling? Good companies very often maintain their competitive advantages for a long time.

- **Holding losers—avoiding regret**

  The opposite of selling winners is not wanting to give up on an investment, because it would be the final admission that you were wrong. Deciding when having conviction in a company is really holding onto a loser is one of the toughest decisions.

- **Illusion of knowledge and control—believing one can control the market**

  Conviction and deep work are great, but investing is about forecasting the future. Forecasting the future is very difficult. You cannot ever have all the information. Equating number of hours worked in a linear fashion with short-term stock selection success is a mistake. There is no sure thing. The most common pitfalls are going to great effort to gain information on an issue that only affects a small part of the business, but believing that specific information ensures a certain outcome. It is also common for the illusion of knowledge to lead an investor to buy very large portfolio positions. Recent information or new analysis may make an investment seem like a sure thing, when in fact it may not be as large a contributing factor to success as believed.

Perfect knowledge is not attainable.

—*George Soros, investor*

- **Reference points—associating the current price with some other past price**

   Using reference points as anchors is a behavioral pitfall that can occur in a variety of ways. The most obvious is when investors hold an investment in an underperforming position until the stock returns to their break-even point. The stock market functions without any knowledge of an individual investor's gains and losses, so there is no reason for that to be part of any investment decision. Focusing on a company's prior high stock price or prior low stock price also has no real relevance to fundamental investment decisions.

- **Fear of risk—avoiding risk to the detriment portfolio goals**

   Losing your clients' (and your own) money creates significant psychological stress. These negative experiences can weigh on portfolio managers to the point that they are avoiding risk in an unwarranted manner. Risk is necessary to achieve returns. Risks have to be understood, but they also have to be accepted.

- **Familiarity—not recognizing options outside your domain**

   This bias directly conflicts with the maxim "invest in what you know," but it is a reminder that the stocks you are involved with may not always be the full set of options and you should keep looking at other opportunities. Familiarity is often an issue with managers, who are sector specific. Focusing deeply in one sector can be informative and productive, but it can also make a manager miss the forest for the trees. The broader market may be signaling issues with a sector, but being deep in the issues of specific companies can cause a manger to miss broader market signals. In bigger firms, trying to avoid this issue is often the role of the portfolio manager in relation to sector analysts.

- **Moods and decisions—emotion-dictating decisions**

   Allowing emotions to come into the decision process can be problematic. Everything from conflicts with investment partners to concerns over the firm's future to personal relationships can cause emotions to get mixed into the decision process. Emotional control is an issue for every investor to recognize and try to manage. This is one of the key reasons to have a defined process and structure that has been thoroughly analyzed and discussed before making investment decisions.

The investor's chief problem—and even his worst enemy—is likely to be himself.

—*Ben Graham, investor*

It is interesting to analyze the decision-making process of private equity and venture capital managers in relation to behavioral issues and performance. Private, illiquid investment managers do not have as many decision points as public managers. They have very defined periods to decide on whether reinvestment makes sense and whether it is time to sell a company, which causes fewer opportunities to make behavioral mistakes. They do not have to watch their investments jump around on a screen every day and have significant price moves both up and down on events that may not pertain to their investment. The lack of liquidity makes them think more often about long-term issues and focus on company and industry specifics.

Venture capital specifically would be almost impossible to manage in a public market environment. Venture capitalists must have huge winners in their portfolio to be successful. Returns on their young companies reach well over 100 times, their initial investment.

Would they be able to hold their best investments for years, if they had the ability to sell each day?

After watching an investment go up over 50 times, it would be difficult not to trim the investment. The explosive growth of venture capital companies and their win/loss rate make rebalancing a very bad idea. Were they to rebalance every quarter or even every year out of their best companies and into their underperforming companies, their returns would suffer significantly. When investing in high-growth companies, this is an important lesson.

All these behavioral pitfalls often contradict each other, which makes knowing when you are making a mistake so difficult.

- When does conviction become **holding losers**?
- When does not being part of the herd mean **selling winners**?
- When does avoiding **familiarity** mean not investing in what you know?
- When does portfolio concentration equate to having an **illusion of control**?

Each is a constant debate. There is a fine balance between a good decision and a bad decision. No one fully avoids these pitfalls, regardless of his or her experience. Recognizing that these issues exist and continuing to learn is the best that can be done.

Trading

Trading from an execution of structural portfolio decisions perspective can be additive to returns. It will not be a huge contributor, but a good trader can be a meaningful contributor. Researching the cheapest trading methods, monitoring total cost analysis, the ability to find block trades when liquidity is an issue, and looking for ways to use cash efficiently are all additive functions. These functions might be best managed by a separate firm trading team, as opposed to an investment strategy function.

Some firms try to add short-term, opportunistic trading to their strategy. This is trading outside the parameters of a defined portfolio management decision to try to add value. Trying to add value through daily and multiday moves is usually a value-destructive exercise for research oriented firms. Some fundamental managers believe they can add value with this type of short-term trading, which is defined here as trading with the expectation to reverse the trade in ten days or less. Their short-term trading thesis usually centers on the belief that they know the companies they invest in better than the market and can take advantage of short-term inefficiencies in the market.

An example often cited is when an investment banking analyst upgrades a portfolio company causing the stock to go up 4% to 5% in a day. The manager may recognize it as an immaterial event, so will sell a portion of the holding to (hopefully) be bought back in a few days when demand dies back down. Trading these short-term daily moves may be seen as an alpha-creating opportunity. There clearly is noise in the market, but it's very difficult to take advantage of in a consistent manner. Understanding a company very well does not mean that you understand the random moves of the market. Rarely have I seen fundamental managers add value consistently by trading short-term market noise and most often they destroy value and create unnecessary distractions.

> *It's just that more than 95% of the trading back and forth each day is probably unnecessary.*
>
> *—Joel Greenblatt, investor*

In analyzing these short-term trading strategies, one should recognize that attribution can be difficult, unless a detailed, systematic attribution plan is put into place. Rules on identifying which lots are short-term trades and reconciling those trades with the appropriate reversal must be put in place. The trades must capture all costs associated with the trading. The most often ignored cost is the opportunity cost. A methodology must be put in place to capture opportunity costs.

If you sell a 5% NAV position down to 4% of NAV on a +5% up day, because an investment banking analyst upgraded the stock and then did not buy the stock back before it went up another 10%, there is an opportunity loss. Every short-term trade has to have an actual reversal or rule of reversal accounting methodology for the attribution to be robust. Rule of reversal accounts for opportunity loss by accounting for the trade reversal in the analysis (i.e. if the trade was not actually reversed after five days then it is assumed to be reversed at that time for the analysis). Many firms do not go to this level of effort to analyze historical attribution. Anecdotal analysis can be misleading.

> *[On share portfolio turnover] Our turnover is very, very low.*
>
> *—Mark Mobius, investor*

The results of this type of short-term trading strategy by fundamental managers fall into three categories from best to worst:

1. **Break-even over years, but nondisruptive.** If the trading function and staff are separate from the research staff and are good traders, they will have a good year or two and then a bad year or two. Over a longer period the attribution contribution will be very close to zero, but there will be no harm to the firm and you hope the traders made enough money to cover their costs, maybe even a little more if they are really good.
2. **Break-even over years, but disruptive.** If the trading function is not separated from the research staff, the focus on trading can be disruptive. The short-term trading may be break-even, but if everyone is sitting around watching computer monitors and talking about the day's trades, there has been no research accomplished. What new portfolio ideas might have been found with the time taken up by trading? What insights might have been understood that would have affected portfolio decisions? You cannot know, but fundamental investment managers should not watch computer screens flash all day.
3. **Money is simply lost.** Short-term trading is random and can cause behavioral trading mistakes that compound on themselves and turn small trades into very material losses.

So if at best a short-term trading strategy can add a little bit of value to your overall strategy, there is no reason to risk large monetary losses or the loss of the focus and culture of the firm.

Should anybody try and execute a short-term trading strategy?

If your strategy and experience are in quantitative or high-frequency trading, then hone your skills and trade. A few of the firms who have a core competency in trading and have significant technology resources and a talented staff can create outperformance. However, there is an important distinction between investing strategies and trading strategies.

Trading strategies (managed by experts) can create outperformance, and it can be repeatable, but one individual trading strategy is not sustainable. Trading strategies work for a few years and then the market competes the advantage away and the strategy no longer works. The trading strategy has to be reinvented every two to five years. An allocator can invest in a trading strategy firm that may be able to repeat its process next year and the year after, but soon the advantage will go away. How do you know when the trading advantage has been lost to the market? When returns go down, but that means you cannot invest with conviction and add monies at opportune times. You need to exit and find another manager when returns drop. This is a much tougher process in allocating capital successfully. Fundamental investing strategies will always have challenges, but they can be both repeatable and sustainable.

Options

Options are the antithesis of many of the key investment tenets discussed. Time horizon has been restricted to be short. The cash flow creation of owning equity is reversed. Investors are paying a fee to limit their time horizon, have less liquidity, and trade inefficiently due to a wide bid/ask spread. Nothing in that statement is positive for an investor.

So given these problems, what is the best course of action?

Don't buy options. Add it to your firm investment strategy: no options. I have never seen a fundamental manager add long-term value through an option strategy.

Why would you buy an option?

The answer is to lever a position that you think will act positively in the short term or hedge a position that concerns you in the short term. If you have to act on one of these issues, both can be managed in a better way than using options. Levering a position you really like short term should be done by buying more of the position and using margin leverage. The margin leverage cost will be cheaper than options. A lot of leverage is not a great idea, but it is better to at least execute your idea in the most cost-efficient manner. If you are really concerned about a position and want to hedge, simply sell some of the position. The only reason that an investor might buy a put option to hedge would be to maintain a share position to achieve long-term tax status (for a taxable investor). A hedge may potentially make sense, if the cost of the option was cheaper than the tax consequence and you felt very compelled to hedge. Otherwise, simply avoiding options is best.

> *The options market is a gigantic, useless, expensive gambling casino.*
> —*Peter Lynch, investor*

Returning to the original thesis of disruption and active investing, portfolio management decisions have been put under stress by the confluence of the two major forces acting on the market today. Stress is created when macro forces outweigh fundamental business results and when technology disruption creates paradigm shifts. This stress drives behavioral mistakes and shortens time horizons. The greatest level of stress has been put on managing a short portfolio, which is discussed in the next chapter.

CHAPTER 12

SHORT INVESTING

- *Why manage a short portfolio*
- *The shorting paradigm and short portfolio management*
- *Quantitatively the risk/reward ratio is different*
- *Short security selection*

If a minority of hedge fund managers have been able to reach their alpha goals this past decade, considerably fewer have added any value through their short portfolio. Unfortunately there is no perfect way to specifically quantify the entire universe of hedge fund managers' short portfolio returns. Anecdotally I would say less than 25% of all hedge fund managers added value through their short portfolio in the 2010s.

Central bank intervention and the longest economic expansion in history have put the vast majority of short-only hedge funds out of business. Many of those that remain have changed their strategy to be market neutral or 50% net short as opposed to 100% net short. Most multibillion-dollar allocators of capital interview a few hundred hedge fund managers every year and monitor hundreds more; today the large capital allocators are probably monitoring less than half a dozen short-only hedge funds.

The 2010s has been the hardest decade to manage a short portfolio in history. From January 2010 to September 2019, the broad US Russell 3000 Index has only had three equity drawdowns greater than 10%, and each time that drawdown was reversed and new highs were seen very quickly. During the decade, the Russell 3000 went longer than seven years without having a 10% drawdown, from 2011 to late 2018. Figure 12.1 illustrates Russell 3000 drawdowns from 2009 to 2019.

The US equity market was strong for the entire decade increasing 13% annually, which is 400 basis points higher than the long-term average. As we have discussed at length central bank intervention and low rates have been the primary driver behind the markets during this period, but the additional difficulty for short portfolio managers has been the continual Fed put. Investors have believed that anytime the market starts to falter the Fed will come in to stem the market slide with further rate cuts or quantitative easing. There seems to be good reason to believe in the Fed put, because Fed governors have reliably found their way to a media event to give a dovish speech

FIGURE 12.1   Russell 3000 drawdowns by month 2009 to October 2019

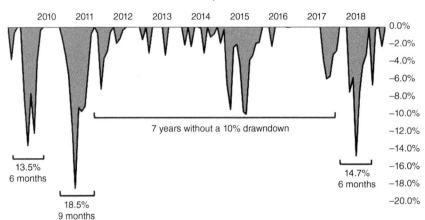

when markets have dropped even 5%. So rates have not only been low but also there has been a continual threat of intervention to support the markets.

Midway through 2019, ten years after the financial crisis with unemployment below 4%, the Fed continues to be willing to do anything to maintain an upward market trend. Many investors feel they have taken on a third mandate of supporting US equity markets, in addition to inflation and unemployment. With all this as a backdrop, many allocators have stopped looking for managers who know how to short, and hedge funds have been using market ETFs to hedge to minimize losses and time spent on short positions. Additionally, many hedge funds are trying to keep their net exposure just low enough to make sure they can still call themselves a hedge fund. Hedge funds usually demand higher fees than long-only managers due to the additional level of complexity and higher expectations in a down market.

Why manage a short portfolio?

Ever the contrarian, I believe managers who know how to create alpha on the short side of their portfolio will be in high demand in the 2020s. The idea and concept of shorting becomes wildly out of favor whenever markets go through these prolonged periods of exuberance. We saw the same trend occur in the late 1990s around the dot-com mania. If you are a younger manager who has been managing a hedge fund for a decade, you most likely see no benefit to putting time and effort into a short portfolio. For ten years, managing a short portfolio has been a skill set that has been relatively ignored and underresearched.

Using market ETFs as a hedging tool has become very common practice in order to avoid short losses and to save time on research. This decision to short ETFs, rather than individual companies, is giving up the opportunity to create alpha in the short portfolio. Hedge funds using ETFs to hedge is a similar thought process to capital allocators moving to passive investment alternatives. When alpha is not being created for a period of time, passive investing is a strong draw. Due to the upward trending markets in the 2010s, hedge fund managers who have used passive alternatives to short may have seemed smart, because many of their peers created negative alpha trying to manage individual company short positions. Passive investing is a good way to stop from creating negative alpha, but it will not be a long-term answer to creating a successful hedge fund. From any sophisticated allocator's standpoint, paying high hedge fund fees to managers using ETFs to short is not cost efficient. They (the allocators) could hedge any long exposure with ETFs themselves and save fees. This lack of short portfolio alpha and use of ETFs by hedge fund managers is another reason for the reallocation of capital to passive investment alternatives. The best course of action today is to prepare for the next decade, not continue practices that made sense last decade. That means spending time on short security selection and designing a short portfolio process that focuses on avoiding the behavioral portfolio mistakes that are the toughest part of shorting.

The reasons to manage a short portfolio are as follows:

- To control volatility (hedge)
- To add alpha—for a hedge fund manager to produce 1,000 basis points of alpha contribution from their short portfolio is necessary
- To aid in the ability to manage your long portfolio well during drawdowns

The shorting paradigm and short portfolio management

Shorting has always been difficult, because you are fighting upstream on an absolute return basis, if you assume the market will provide a positive equity risk premium over time, which it always has over ten-year periods. The first thing a manager has to recognize and embrace is that managing a short portfolio is very different than managing a long portfolio. Security selection is not the most difficult part of making money on the short side of the portfolio. Portfolio management of the positions selected is the major cause of losses. After analyzing the short performance history of hundreds of managers, the attribution highlights two major problems: **no large winners** and **potential for extraordinarily large losers.**

The first problem is there will be no large long-term winners, as there will be in the long portfolio. Many positions produce small gains or losses even when security selection is quite good. This is simply due to the mathematical inability to make over 100% on the buy and hold of a single position. The best an individual position can probably add is 70% to 80% upside. You cannot compound returns on a single security over long periods of time the way you can on the long side.

The second problem is there can be big losers. It is very common to see one or two positions destroy the returns of an entire short portfolio. For golfers the analogy is playing 16 great holes, but scoring triple bogeys on two holes destroying the round. Shorting is a constant struggle to avoid those one or two positions that destroy the year's short alpha.

Given that portfolio management is more important than security selection in creating short alpha, we will start there and then discuss individual short security selection issues. Fundamental equity managers who inherently believe in many of the concepts we have been discussing, such as high portfolio concentration and buying with conviction, need to destroy their belief that a short portfolio can be managed in the same fashion. Although short security selection may often be the reverse of long security selection, a short portfolio cannot be managed the same way as a long portfolio.

Quantitatively the risk reward ratio is different

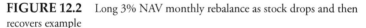

Rebalancing a long portfolio by selling a portion of the portfolio winners and buying the portfolio losers is generally a benefit to returns in a public portfolio. On the short side it cannot be done this way systematically.

In Figure 12.2 a 3% NAV long portfolio position in a $20 stock is purchased and over the next 18 months the stock drops to $4 and recovers in a normal distribution; that doesn't happen, but it makes for an easy example to understand. If the position were never touched the simple return would be zero. By rebalancing

FIGURE 12.2   Long 3% NAV monthly rebalance as stock drops and then recovers example

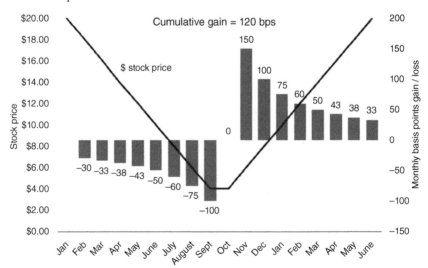

(buying more of the underperforming stock) to 3% of the portfolio NAV every month, the long position makes +120 basis points of profit. The stock went down 80% from $20 to $4, but then went up 400% from $4 to $20. If you bought on the way down and maintained the same NAV percentage each month, you were compensated for your conviction and made money in a break-even scenario.

What if a similar conviction buying philosophy was used in short portfolio management?

Figure 12.3 illustrates a 3% NAV short position that started at $20 and every time the position went up (against you) 30%, the manager added 1.0% to the position. Shorting with conviction in your thesis. The problem is there is no upside ceiling and at $42, the 3.0% short NAV position had lost the fund 433 bps. Short positions rise in value (as a % of NAV) when the stock is moving the wrong way, unlike long positions that hurt less and less as they go down. This means in a short portfolio you are constantly fighting against momentum and momentum is a strong factor in equity markets. When the losses are compounding this fast and there is no reason the stock cannot keep going up, conviction becomes stubbornness, because you are risking the alpha of the fund for the entire year on this one position.

- If the stock goes to $55 and a year later back to $20, did you really win the battle?
- How many investors have you lost in the process?
- What was the effect of the losses on other decisions in the portfolio

As an aside, if you think the 100% move in the illustration is uncommonly large for one year, on average about 5% of all stocks in the Russell 3000 will be up 100+%

FIGURE 12.3   Short 3% NAV adding exposure on the way up example

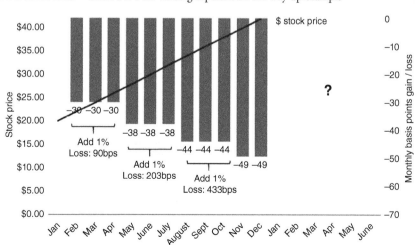

at some point during the year and another 10%, 15% cumulatively, will go up 50+% at some point during the year. Large single-stock intra-year gains are not uncommon, even in low return market years. There is too much to lose to short with conviction in a process similar to the long portfolio methodology. That does not mean you cannot short as the position goes up a little, but if in the short term you are not proven right, you need to give up and cover some of your position. That mentality is stated nowhere else in this book: "think in the short term … and give up." The behavioral mistakes of portfolio management discussed before are multiplied many times over in managing a short portfolio. You need to recognize how your defined short portfolio management process will create behavioral stress.

Reviewing an example, where a short position was working well and then reversed, it is also clear rebalancing is not advantageous. In Figure 12.4, the same price movement example is used as the prior long position in Figure 12.2, but this example demonstrates the difference in being short the stock. The stock drops from $20 to $4 and then recovers. If we are short and just let the NAV fluctuate with the stock price then the simple return is zero. If we rebalance every month to maintain the NAV position at 3%, we produce **a loss of 120 basis points** (compared to the 120 basis point gain in a long position). Same security selection, same portfolio management, completely different outcome. To sophisticated short sellers this may be obvious, but continually reminding yourself of this breaks the reaction to manage a short position in the same way you would a long position.

I hope these examples are convincing enough to break the illusion that a short portfolio can be managed in similar fashion to a long portfolio. Once it is accepted

FIGURE 12.4   Short 3% NAV monthly rebalance as stock drops and then recovers example

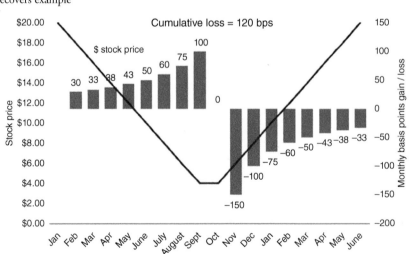

that short portfolio management is different, we can begin to build an entirely different process.

Because of the quantitative performance issues discussed, there will have to be many more small gains taken in the portfolio and more capitulation. When a short position produces a 25% gain and has a strong balance sheet, it may be time to cover and move on to another idea. On average, good short positions offer a gain of 25%, whereas bad positions can cause a 50+% loss. This is a 1:2 win/loss return ratio, with the odds on the side of the loss. This is an important realization; the risk/reward ratio of a short investment is very often the reverse of a long investment. Researching a company on the long side of the portfolio and projecting a potential win/loss return ratio of 2:1 is very common.

Because the risk/reward ratio is different, there will be **more trading**, **more reinvestment risk**, and **more work per dollar** invested in the short portfolio. The increased trading comes from trimming positions that are moving higher (against the manager) and trimming positions that are dropping and making money, but getting closer to a value that makes the short investment uncompelling.

Reinvestment risk is important to recognize. You need to short and cover positions at a much faster pace than in a long portfolio, so you have to have new ideas ready. A disciplined process of price targets and idea generation is a necessity for a short portfolio manager. It is possible to be in and out of the same company for years on the short side if you believe it is a flawed business model. Unfortunately, you cannot simply hold the flawed business model company, because at times it will be uncompelling due to valuation or market environment. It is often relatively easy to find companies that are being disrupted and will eventually disappear, but they are not always easy to short and make money. The flawed business model company may have potential acquirers, they may have new management teams excite investors for a turnaround, or they may negotiate desperate partnerships to keep the company alive. All these things can make the stock price spike from very low valuation levels and cause material losses.

As an example, if a hedge fund manager had researched Abercrombie & Fitch in December 2009 and decided it was a flawed business model due to e-commerce taking market share, malls no longer being a meeting place for teens, and brand deterioration, they would have been correct. Demonstrated in Figure 12.5, the stock has returned −53% since 2009 compared to the S&P 500 +220%. Choosing a stock that underperforms the index by 270% is great security selection.

Unfortunately over the ten-year period that the stock dropped 53%, there were periods of very large upside performance (losses to a short seller). In 2010 the economy was recovering and almost all cheap retailers went up as investors were wildly anticipating a consumer recovery. The macroeconomic news of the day overwhelmed any individual company research and Abercrombie & Fitch rose 123%. Over the next eight years, as your thesis was being proven completely correct, the stock went up over 30% four times. On a quarterly basis, there were 39 quarterly periods and the stock was up in 22 of the periods, so the stock was up more than it was down on a quarterly

FIGURE 12.5   Abercrombie & Fitch (ANF) short example 2009 to Q3 2019

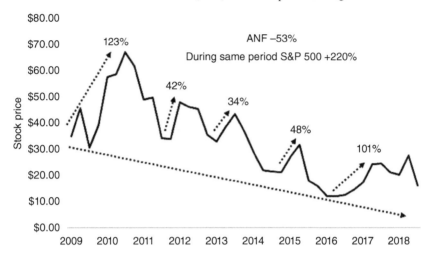

basis despite a 53% overall loss. This is a very common scenario for good shorts in a strong market environment. When the company reports news, the stock drops, but in between those news releases the general market grinds higher taking the stock with it. Timing and portfolio management are clearly much more important on the short side of the portfolio than security selection. Many managers lose money despite good short security selection.

Given all these challenges and idiosyncratic risks, such as buy-outs, management changes, and new partnerships, what are the keys to being successful in managing a short portfolio?

- **Concentrate the portfolio less.** Tending toward more equal-weight NAV positions is better than large NAV variances. Managers often think that they can prioritize their investments and have insight into which should be larger portfolio positions. On the long side, that may be true. On the short side it is more difficult, because results are more short-term focused. Any stock, whether good or bad, can have a big price spike due to some factor that no one can see coming. This means that holding an outsized position can cause real problems affecting decisions across the portfolio.

- **Diversify considering fundamental short themes.** Holding multiple positions with a similar short thesis will avoid buy-out and other idiosyncratic risks. Obviously, you don't want to short a company you like or think is very cheap, but if you think a certain retailer is a good short then step back and think about whether the reasons for that short are applicable to other retailers. It may be possible to diversify the idiosyncratic risk by shorting three or four retailers at smaller NAV levels. All else being equal, three weak retailers at 2% NAV each is better than one at 6% NAV due to the challenges of shorting.

- **Do not rebalance systematically.** A number of examples have been discussed, but the concept of rebalancing and investing with conviction is different in managing a short portfolio.
- **Don't be stubborn when positions go against you.** Risking all the other work being done due to one position in the short portfolio going up 200% is not worth the potential reward. The risk of large losses is too great to be stubborn in the way that may make sense with positions in the long portfolio.
- **Create a disciplined short portfolio management process.** Behavioral mistakes are amplified in managing the short portfolio, so process and investing discipline are even more important. The exact process will be dependent on the overall strategy and needs to complement the long portfolio structure and recognize the portfolio and manager risk tolerance limits.

So consider the original question, Why manage a short portfolio given the challenges?

It should be stressed again that the 2010s have been abnormally difficult due to central bank intervention. Shorting is always difficult, but it has been next to impossible during this decade. Many managers have given up shorting or are not spending any time on short research today. This level of difficulty will change in the next decade. Slow growth and peak margins will pressure earnings. Volatility will increase, because central bank intervention will not be as productive in the 2020s. Central bank intervention will either fail due to investor's concern over the size of the intervention or will become less effective simply because it cannot be increased to the same degree it was increased last decade.

A great reason to manage a short portfolio is to support the decision-making process of the long portfolio. All the investment tenets that add value in the long portfolio are easier to execute if you have a short portfolio creating gains in times of stress. The tenets of being a contrarian, taking large concentrated positions, needing a long time horizon, and buying when your favorite companies are down all become challenging in times of stress. The short portfolio can lessen the stress and enable good decisions. The number one way to really outperform is to take advantage of dislocations and be a buyer, when the market has turned to *fear* rather than *greed*. It is much easier to be a buyer, if you have not lost large amounts of capital during the dislocation. Managing a short portfolio to win in periods of market stress and not hurt too much in strong market environments can be a great benefit to overall returns.

Short security selection

Although short portfolio management is very different from the long portfolio, security selection on the short side can more closely resemble the mirror opposite of long security selection. You would like to find companies with balance sheet leverage, declining sales and declining margins. The process of having a compelling investment thesis before entering the position and tracking results versus that thesis are exactly the same. A few nuances and areas to focus on are detailed next. Many of the key issues center on shorter-term timing issues and catalysts.

Market perception. In selecting short positions you need to understand the market's perception of the company more so than with a long position. An understanding of what the market is discounting in the stock is always important, but market perception needs additional attention when time horizons are shorter. Short-term catalysts become a bigger part of the investment thesis. If a poor company is losing market share, but it is expected and the company has a strong balance sheet and is trading at a 7% free cash flow yield, it may not be a great short. If your research and perception of the company are not that different from the market's perception, you may want to wait until there is a better entry point or a shorter term catalyst that you expect to occur.

Balance sheet. The balance sheet has to be a point of focus for any short. If a company has a net cash position and is not significantly burning cash, the short sale return expectation has to reflect the downside support a strong balance sheet will provide. Strong balance sheets are the reason buying with conviction works in the long portfolio, but in the short portfolio they are a reason companies, even bad companies, get support or are bought out.

Finding a company that is a good short candidate and has balance sheet leverage is great. The reason is simple, the value of the company does not have to go to zero for the equity price result to be zero. If you short a $10 billion company with $10 billion of debt, the value of the company only needs to drop 50% for the equity price to go to zero. Finding a company with a combination of both leverage and volatile margins makes for a particularly good short candidate. Any dislocation in the company's marketplace or recessionary scare will hurt the company more than the rest of the market. Investors will enter new sales and margin expectations into their models and recognize that the combination of a drop in EV/EBITDA and a drop in EBITDA margins at the same time is powerful. In prior chapters, we discussed the downside to investing in capex-intensive companies. These capex-intensive companies can be great short positions at the end of cycles, when the supply of assets has grown to meet demand and markets have forgotten the pain of down cycles.

Valuation. Valuation is one of the toughest issues in short security selection. At the extremes, valuation does *not* matter and should *not* be part of the investment thesis. Generally, this is when a company is in the first (highest valued) and tenth (lowest valued) valuation deciles. Figure 12.6 shows a chart of the Russell 3000 price/sales ratio by decile. You can see that the average price to sales ratio of the second decile is 7.0 times. These levels vary by year, but generally the maximum valuation in the second decile is nine to ten times price to sales. If a company is trading over nine to ten times sales, valuation is not a factor that the market or analysts are concerned about in regards to the investment. They will pay whatever it takes to own the company and there is no difference between 12 times sales and 16 times sales, because neither one is grounded in any kind of quantitative financial

FIGURE 12.6 Russell 3000 price/sales multiples by decile

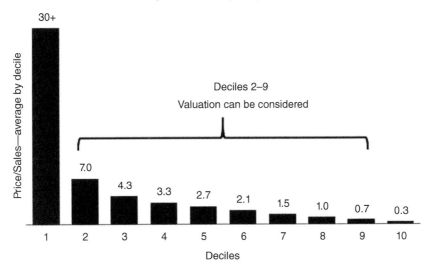

Source: Author adapted from FTSE Russell data.

valuation analysis. Valuations that high are about stories, so the short investment thesis has to be about the story and how it will change, not about valuation. Recognize issues such as analyst coverage and popular media will then be a large part of the near-term future, because those factors are the drivers of stories and first decile valuation stocks.

On the other end of the spectrum (tenth decile), if a company is trading at less than 0.5 times sales, there is probably nothing left worth shorting. Any number of factors could make the stock go up significantly. The company could be bought, a new management team could excite investors, or a new debt package could be approved. Valuation again is not part of the story. A potential reorganization or new beginning is the focus.

Valuation as a short position catalyst is often difficult because a company can maintain high valuations for a long time. If a company is trading at 16 times EV/EBITDA and 12 times EV/EBITDA makes sense, it can be a long time until the market agrees. If you do have a catalyst, it can be a particularly good short, because the multiple will de-rate as the earnings drop making the decline larger.

When adding valuation as a focus in the investment thesis, recognize there is usually some non-company-specific factor that is driving the high valuation. For example, the market may love SaaS companies or central bank–driven low rates are spurring demand for dividend-paying utility companies. In these situations, it is best to have some thesis around why that factor may change. Additionally, when valuation is a driver behind the investment thesis, it can be an opportunity to diversify across other similar companies. Usually if one SaaS company, auto retailer, or energy company is historically expensive, its peers are also expensive at the same time.

> *Overvaluation is not always apparent to investors, analysts, or managements. Since security prices reflect investors' perception of reality and not necessarily reality itself, overvaluation may persist for a long time.*
>
> —*Seth Klarman, investor*

Battleground stocks and borrow costs. Somewhat similar to story-driven, high-valuation stocks are *battleground* stocks. Battleground stocks are those stocks that every hedge fund is tracking and has an opinion on and the investment news media covers constantly. Half the market hates the stock and the other half loves it, and the company is being talked about in the hallway of every investment conference. Even if you have an opinion, the investment has a high likelihood of wearing you out, as it bounces up and down in a volatile fashion every day. Avoiding these companies lowers behavioral mistakes and saves research time.

Additionally, these companies often have high borrow costs, which should be a focus for any short portfolio manager. An area where many managers could add value is simply by analyzing their short borrow costs continually and bidding the trades out across their trading partners. There is a lot of money left on the table by managers paying more than they need to in borrow costs, which is proven by the short borrow divisions of investment banks being large profit centers.

There have been numerous academic papers written on the performance of high borrow cost stocks in relation to the overall market. Some of the papers find that high borrow cost stocks underperform the market and other papers find the opposite. The issue is difficult due to the different ways you can define the methodology for the analysis (time period, definition of what high borrow means, etc.). Anecdotally, I have never seen a manager succeed with a consistent process of being short high borrow cost stocks. Although the companies are often very highly valued, fads, or potential frauds and may underperform over time, the difficulty in the portfolio management/trading of these stocks often leads to failure. The failure is a combination of higher volatility causing behavioral mistakes, the high borrow cost eating away at returns, and potentially a lack of good firm research that causes the firm short portfolio to consistently hold stocks that everyone is talking about and already short.

Negative momentum. Stocks with negative momentum are often better short candidates. Previously the predictive power of valuation over time was discussed. The analysis showed that over long periods of time, valuation is very predictive. Over shorter periods of time, such as one or two years, valuation does not have much predictive power. In shorter time periods, momentum is more predictive of returns than valuation. Shorting stocks with negative momentum is more productive than shorting stocks with high valuations in a one-year analysis. For this reason, shorting stocks with negative momentum is advantageous. Momentum tends to maintain its trend in short periods and negative momentum helps avoid the big losses that can hurt performance. Big short sale losses often occur as momentum investors buy and ignore valuation.

Expectations. The best way to manage a short portfolio is bring your return expectations and risk tolerance down. Focus on not allowing a short position to ruin all the other work in the portfolio. When managers try to add large levels of alpha through holding 10% NAV short positions, it is often counterproductive. Set an alpha goal in the 300 to 400 basis points per year range, which is less than the long portfolio goal. It only makes sense that the challenges of shorting should make it a more difficult path to creating alpha; don't overreach. The goal of reaching 1,000 basis points of alpha overall can still be achieved with only a 300–400 basis point contribution from the short portfolio. By trying to achieve 1,000 basis points of alpha in the short portfolio alone, there is a high likelihood that negative alpha will be created hurting the entire portfolio. If a manager reaches 1,000 basis points of alpha per year, performance will be in the top decile of hedge fund managers.

More work. In creating a successful short portfolio management process, it must be recognized that even though short portfolio return expectations are lower, the amount of research work done on short positions cannot be lower. In fact, managing a short portfolio takes more time than managing a long portfolio, because there is more trading and turnover. More short investments move in and out of the portfolio, which means more companies to be researched. There is no way to take shortcuts. Managing a short portfolio is more time for less return, and a good process recognizes that issue.

During the 2010s, central bank–driven low volatility and low rates have decimated the ranks of short-only hedge funds and pushed many other hedge funds to use ETFs to hedge. Hedge fund managers have stopped spending research time and honing their skills in managing individual short positions due to the relentless upward trend of the markets. The 2020s will have more than three 10% drawdowns and volatility will increase, so shorting should not be a forgotten craft.

PART III

THE BIGGER PICTURE

Goal congruence, fiduciary responsibility, and continual learning are at the foundation of investment management and business generally. Each is needed before any of the other best practices in managing an investment firm can be applied successfully to sustain value over time.

> *Trust is congruence between what you say and what you do.*
>
> —*Peter Drucker, management educator*

Change is a constant in business and investing, which makes continual learning the foundation of success. With the incredible amount of data in the world today, learning has to be managed proactively. Stepping back and thinking about what you want to learn and how to find the right resources is as important as having the desire to learn.

> *Read 500 pages like this every day. That's how knowledge works. It builds up, like compound interest. All of you can do it, but I guarantee not many of you will do it.*
>
> —*Warren Buffett, investor*

I have used quotes liberally in this section from investors much more successful than I have ever been to convince you of the merits of these foundational issues.

CHAPTER 13

GOAL CONGRUENCE, FIDUCIARY RESPONSIBILITY, AND LEARNING

- *Executive compensation and board structure*
- *Assets under management (AUM) and fee structures*
- *Corporate acquisition conflicts*
- *Country regulatory issues*
- *Learning*

Goal congruence and trust are the foundation that all other investment tenets need to build on. A simple statement, but it is important to recognize its value when doing early due diligence. Goal congruence has to be managed and understood whether it be an allocator's relationship with an investment manager, an investment manager's relationship with a company management team, or any business relationship. Recognizing this fact can be a great time saver, because additional due diligence time does not need to occur if you cannot get past this first hurdle.

From an allocator's perspective, if a manager is not totally transparent and interested in spending the time to educate a new limited partner on his or her process and business practices, there is really no reason to consider the capital allocation.

From a public investor's perspective, if there are serious questions on accounting credibility, management honesty, or conflicting relationships, there is no reason to spend time on further research. In the public markets, there is a lot of regulatory oversight and investor focus, so not many companies fall into the absolute lack of fiduciary responsibility category, but about 1% of the universe can be excluded as simply bad actors. The beauty of public investing is that you have a liquid alternative and many options. In the private equity arena, it is harder to exit, which should mean you spend that much more time thinking about goal congruence and trust prior to investing. Skipping this first foundational step is forgetting the forest for the trees.

Sometimes the lack of goal congruence and fiduciary responsibility is apparent, but there are quite a few gray areas. You may generally have goal congruence with management, but have specific unavoidable conflicts that need to be monitored or a conflict may evolve where there was none in the past. A few examples that are important to monitor are discussed in the following sections.

Executive compensation and board structure

Executive compensation is an interesting issue. Individual investors need to determine where they draw the line on compensation being peer competitive and incentivizing versus egregious and self-serving. Some investors feel that compensation can be as high as possible, as long as it is stock option based and the management team is only making money when the stock is going up and shareholders are participating in the success. Stock option–based compensation is a good tool, but it can go too far, because equity dilution is always an issue for investors. Executives may exercise options at high prices diluting shareholders, only to have the stock price drop the next year, so the executives were compensated for stock appreciation that did not last for the shareholder.

Base salaries should generally be in line with industry benchmarks and incentive compensation should be the most important element, but the incentive metrics have to be well designed. It is a natural tendency for people to manage to compensation metrics, and there are many cases of poorly designed incentive metrics causing real problems in a company. Compensation incentive metrics should be one of the board's most important functions and a capital allocator's focus in hiring an investment manager. Although there are entire books written on designing incentive compensation, the key is goal congruence among all the constituents: executives, employees, and shareholders. This is easier said than done and takes a very involved board that has a vision for the future of the company and understands the implications of focusing on growth, profitability, or stock return metrics.

Why do egregious compensation packages get approved by boards?

Many boards (and investors) fall under the spell of personal charisma. They come to believe that there is only one person who can guide their company to success. In most cases, that is not true. There are clear examples of executive visionaries such as Steve Jobs and Jeff Bezos, but they are the outliers, not the norm. Many executives given huge compensation packages amounting to tens of millions of dollars annually could and probably would work for much less, but boards are scared of losing them based on their past successes, personal charisma, and the comfort of management continuity. Most public companies are rightly built on brands, technology, and distribution channels, not on the individual talents of one person. If a company CEO is truly seen as irreplaceable, the business has more problems than the compensation plan being too large.

Management is very important, but success or failure is often driven by timing and change in an industry. As a minority investor in a public company, you may not have much influence on management changes and compensation packages, but watching the decisions made and the process can be enlightening to the culture and direction of the company.

Board structure is, also, a key issue. When you have a company that has conflicts among its shareholders or the company is embarking on a major strategic turnaround or acquisition, board members and corporate structure take on heightened importance. Often when you become very concerned about board structure and company management not being receptive to changing or adding directors from the outside, it is a sign that you should move on to another investment. There are always companies with major board and insider ownership turmoil that have assets that are being undervalued. In my experience, these investments in great assets, but internal turmoil, are frustrating and not productive. You can be correct about the value of the assets, but end up being worn out over time by the company turmoil and exit at the wrong time. The board or major shareholder problems can also destroy value by spending time on their internal issues and ignoring the company operations and industry.

Assets under management (AUM) and fee structures

For capital allocators (limited partners), a natural conflict is the size of an investment firm's assets under management and its fee structure. In the prior discussion on fund strategy, one important piece was the relationship among the strategy, its liquidity, and the assets under management. It is very natural for a manager to want to build assets. More assets means more fees, but there comes a point where the manager's desire to build assets and an investor's potential returns come into conflict. Analyzing and understanding the level of assets where this conflict becomes a real issue is very important. All managers will think they can manage more assets without returns deteriorating than they probably can, so allocators need to lead this discussion and know at what asset level they should divest. This may be a very honest disagreement on the part of the manager and allocator and not a breach of fiduciary responsibility by the manager, but it is still a goal congruence conflict.

> *[On AUM size:] The question is what more assets gets you. Maybe more fees for the manager. But it doesn't necessarily make the investor more money.*
> —*David Tepper, investor*

Many managers recognize the asset size limitations of their strategy and close their fund, but then start working on a new strategy and new fund to allow the firm to keep accepting new monies and collect more fees. This may be a different conflict in that the manager's time is now being divided by multiple fund strategies and new fund-raising activities. Managers need to make sure they have goal congruence with their original clients by communicating how these new strategies are beneficial to them. Transparency and open dialogue are the best paths to avoiding conflicts.

The amount of personal capital a manager (general partner) has in the fund is obviously a factor in creating goal congruence, but it can be a delicate balance. It may seem that the best amount of personal capital investment managers have in their fund from a capital allocator (limited partner) perspective would be *everything,* but that is not always the case. There can be a point at which investment managers have so much of their personal capital in the fund that they begin making more risk-averse decisions than the investors (limited partners) may want.

If capital allocators have 50 different investment/hedge fund managers in their portfolio, they should not want every fund to be managed with the most risk-averse strategy possible. The capital allocator risk is lowered significantly through the diversification of managers. Investment managers who have 100% of their personal wealth in their fund with no outside liquidity may feel pressure beyond what is necessary and be forced into risk averse decisions for personal reasons. Fund managers will always, and should, take on higher personal risk in relation to their fund than capital allocators, but there becomes a point where the idea of skin in the game to create goal congruence becomes detrimental to optimal fund decisions.

From my experience watching managers, I think the optimal amount of personal capital for investment managers to have in their fund is between 50% and 80% of their net worth. Goal congruence is created when managers have a majority of their net worth in the fund, while pushing beyond 80% can create risk averse decisions that are not optimal.

Corporate acquisition conflicts

As an investor, acquisitions can create goal congruence conflicts. Management may be incentivized to grow the company and acquisitions are often the quickest avenue to growth, but they come with a number of risks. The price paid for an acquisition may not be as important to the acquiring management team as it should be. Management may have growth compensation incentives that do not account for the cost of that growth or may have visions of building empires that are more grandiose than practical. The conflict does not have to be driven by irrationality in any way; it is often simply because the acquirers are truly excited about the potential and overproject the potential synergies and success of the acquisition. As mentioned, the success of acquisitions has been studied using different methodologies and with somewhat different findings. Specifically from an acquisition price perspective the majority of studies have shown that the price paid for an acquisition (sales or earnings multiple) is not a clear determinant of eventual success or failure. Intuitively, you would think price would be a major determinant, but it is a tough thing to analyze. High-growth companies can receive very high valuations and be successful and dying companies can be acquired at bargain prices and be failures. Some acquisitions can be very expensive, but be successful due to synergies with the acquiring company, and in some cases those synergies may never be attained.

Again, as a minority investor, you may have very little influence on acquisition decisions, but analyzing how they are made, how often they are made, and doing due diligence on the transitions and success are extremely important in understanding the company and grading management teams.

Country regulatory issues

Government regulation and tax changes are a part of investing everywhere, but some jurisdictions and sectors face an increased risk of conflict that investors need to monitor and handicap. The management team you are investing with may be very honest and have goal congruence with its investors, but the country they operate in may not have the same goal congruence. This issue is most prominent in emerging market countries, but you could extend it to encompass regulatory bodies in developed countries that are at odds with specific companies or industries. These issues become very political and difficult to predict.

Countries that are under stress financially or politically often go to their corporate citizens to extract rents. Utility companies in emerging market countries are a common source of funds for struggling governments, and some countries have a long history of changing licensing and taxation laws every five to ten years. When deficits grow or cash is needed to fund populist agendas, increasing taxes or concessions on regulated companies, such as utilities and banks, is an easy solution. Investors have to handicap this potential hit to the projected cash flows of their investment. It makes many emerging market country regulated companies hard to own, when you know they are performing well above their cost of capital, because the government also sees their financial success and is attracted to the cash.

Many egregious examples, such as Russian oil companies trading at five times P/E due to their clear government involvement or corruption are not worth the time. If the dividend yields are high enough, you may exit the investment with a positive return, but it has been time spent on an investment that you know will not drive long-term sustained outperformance.

Learning

One of the undeniable business truths is that change is constant. Continual learning is the best answer to proactively managing change positively and being well prepared to overcome change when it is negative.

In the short term, the value of learning can be difficult to quantify, but in the long term the value of learning becomes obvious. In an analysis of successful investment managers and business executives, learning was broken down into specific traits. Reading voraciously, being curious, interacting with peers, recognizing patterns, and acknowledging mistakes are some of the most important traits to try and emulate.

Successful investors read voraciously to try and gain insights into their universe of companies, investing principles, and the markets in general. This quest for knowledge is a trait that has been cited repeatedly by successful investors. Because there is only so much time in a day, it is important to step back and think strategically about what you read and how much time you can allocate to each issue.

> *It is important to be a voracious reader. Reading is like your body's muscles; use it or lose it.*
>
> —*Mark Mobius, investor*

In order to continue learning and reading, you have to be curious and interested in the subject. Anyone can force themselves to read and study for a short period of time, but no one can force him- or herself to read and acquire knowledge for decades. Your curiosity and interest will pervade your firm's process in a very positive manner.

> *The successful investor is usually an individual who is inherently interested in business problems.*
>
> —*Philip Fisher, investor*

Interest and curiosity have to be mixed with the ability to be proactive. The desire to go out and find new ideas and research new companies cannot be diminished. Someone who turns over 1,000 rocks will be more successful than someone who turns over 100 rocks. At each step of the due diligence process being interested and curious about why different businesses and strategies work the way they do will lead to long-term success.

> *You can't wait for inspiration. You have to go after it with a club.*
>
> —*Jack London, author*

Interacting with partners, peers, and clients is another great educational source. Successful managers like to hear the bear case to their favorite investments, because it makes them look at the investment from a different angle. Talking about past mistakes and new ideas with peers is always a learning experience. Some investment managers cite concerns about sharing proprietary information. While there may be specific instances, such as entering a new investment or a crowded short position, when discretion is advised having an ideology that isolates oneself from other investors and does not share ideas and lessons learned would be more detrimental to you than to your peers. They are missing out on one data point (yours); you are missing out on multiple data points (all of theirs). An investor has more to learn than to lose from others.

I stress-tested my opinions by having the smartest people I could find challenge them so I could find out where I was wrong.

—*Ray Dalio, investor*

Pattern recognition is very important in the investment management business. Think about events and outcomes and how and why they fit together. Absolutes don't occur in investing or business, but there are certain events that signal outcomes. Investing has been described as a mosaic many times. It's not just looking at a static mosaic and trying to see the answer. It is a mosaic that is unfolding in front of you over time in a pattern of data. The pattern unfolds like a game show question; if you see 20% of the mosaic and buzz in with your guess and are wrong you are out, but if you have to wait until all the clues are given, someone else will have beaten you to the answer. Being in before others and having the ability to see the true value is a big advantage, but getting into investments too fast will cause poor selection. Doing analysis from as many vantage points as possible and learning from history is the best course of action.

Last, your own mistakes are the best learning tools. You will take them to heart more than any other data points. Don't push losses or bad decisions out of your mind; acknowledge the existence of mistakes. Do case studies on bad decisions, discuss them with the team, and analyze the time line of events from as many angles as possible.

You have to screw up a bunch and learn from it.

—*Joel Greenblatt*

Growing as an investor is learning to be better prepared to make the next decision. Work to be an independent thinker who can recognize patterns, foresee change, and manage your emotions throughout the investment process.

GLOSSARY

Active investing: Making decisions on investments with the goal of beating the market.

Alpha: A measure of risk-adjusted performance in comparison to a benchmark. Alpha can be thought of as the excess return of an individual stock or portfolio after it has been adjusted for risk. Risk in this case is defined as the volatility of the investment in comparison to the benchmark. Beta, a measure of the volatility in comparison to the benchmark, is used to risk adjust the excess return creating the performance measurement, alpha.

Basis point (bps): One one-hundredth of a percent; 0.01%.

Beta: (Actual definition): A measure of the volatility (systematic risk) of a stock in comparison to an index. From a statistical perspective, beta is the slope of the line through a regression of the individual stock return and index return data points. A beta of 1.0 represents a stock (or group of stocks) that has the same volatility as the market. A beta greater than 1.0 represents higher volatility than the market, and a beta of below 1.0 represents lower volatility than the market.

(Alternative definition): A term that represents a certain type of market exposure. Sometimes it is termed an "emerging markets beta," by which is meant to add stocks that capture a return similar to the emerging markets index.

Central bank intervention: The process of a country's central bank being active in financial markets. Traditionally influencing interest rates through market activities, buying and selling their country's sovereign bonds, but increasingly growing to involvement in other financial assets.

Correlation: The degree of relationship between different assets in a portfolio. A correlation of 1.0 means assets move in tandem and a correlation of −1.0 means they move in opposite directions. Used to understand diversification and risk in a portfolio.

Equity risk premium: The variance in return of an equity to the risk-free rate. Specifically, it can be calculated in a number of ways, but conceptually it should be thought of as the excess return received by an investor for taking the risk of owning an equity versus the risk-free rate.

Excess return: An individual stock or portfolios return compared to that of a benchmark.

Exchange traded fund (ETF): An investment vehicle created to track an underlying index. Different ETF funds may have different investment holdings depending on which geographic or sector index they are trying to replicate. Investing in ETFs is a form of passive investing.

Goal congruence: The alignment of goals between two or more parties.

Gross exposure and net exposure: Gross exposure is the total amount of investment obligations you have in relation to your equity base (assets under management). For a hedge fund it includes both long and short exposure added together. With $100 in equity (AUM), a hedge fund owns $120 in stock (120% long) and has sold short $100 in stock (100% short); the gross exposure is 220%. The net exposure is the difference between the long and short exposure. 120% − 100% = 20% net exposure in this example.

Leverage: Leverage can be used in a number of different ways. *Company balance sheet leverage* is the level of debt that a company holds in relation to some other financial metric (assets, EBITDA, market cap). *Portfolio leverage* is the level of investment exposure versus the assets under management; owning $120 of stock, when you have $100 in your portfolio is 20% leverage. *Income statement leverage* is the increase in margin (gross, operating, or net) that is achieved by adding an additional dollar of sales.

Momentum: From an investment perspective, assets that have had high relative performance returns versus the overall market over the past 3 or 12 months.

Paradigm shift: Fundamental or structural change; not a temporary variance.

Passive investing: Buying the market ETFs that exactly replicate stock market indices. Investing with the goal of accepting the general market return.

Risk: Quantitatively defined as volatility. The broader qualitative definition of risk in investment portfolios can encompass many factors, such as geographic, sector, and market cap diversification, exposure to global currencies or commodities, and so on. An investor can never truly understand all the risks in an investment, but analyzing an investment from every perspective is the goal.

Short (stock): The sale of an asset that you do not own executed by borrowing the stock from a counterparty with the obligation to buy it back at some time in the future. An investor that shorts a stock hopes to buy it back at a lower price in the future.

Systematic risk: Risk inherent to the entire market, as opposed to the additive risk of an individual stock or portfolio decision.

Volatility: Quantitative measurement of risk. The statistical dispersion/variance of returns of a security. The market volatility can be seen through the Volatility Index (or VIX)

INDEX